March

BEYOND PROZAC

HEALING MENTAL SUFFERING WITHOUT DRUGS

To my wife, Mary, my two boys, Gary and David,
and loved ones near and far

First published in 2001 by Marino Books
An imprint of Mercier Press
16 Hume Street Dublin 2
Tel (01) 661 5299; Fax (01) 661 8583
E.mail: books@marino.ie
Trade enquiries to CMD Distribution
55A Spruce Avenue
Stillorgan Industrial Park
Blackrock County Dublin
Tel: (01) 294 2556; Fax: (01) 294 2564
E.mail:cmd@columba.ie

© Dr Terry Lynch 2001
© Foreword Dr Tony Humphreys 2001

ISBN 1 86023 136 5

10 9 8 7 6 5 4 3 2

A CIP record for this title is available
from the British Library

Cover design by Penhouse Design
Printed in Ireland by ColourBooks,
Baldoyle Industrial Estate, Dublin 13

BEYOND PROZAC

HEALING MENTAL SUFFERING WITHOUT DRUGS

DR TERRY LYNCH

FOREWORD BY DR TONY HUMPHREYS

COPYRIGHT AKNOWLEDGEMENTS

Grateful acknowledgement is made to the following authors and publishers for permission to reproduce extracts from copyright material:

HarperCollins Publishers Ltd for Dorothy Rowe's foreword to *Against Therapy* by Jeremy Masson (1997); Pelican Books for *Sanity, Madness and the Family* by R. D. Laing and A. Esterson (1970); Routledge for *Users and Abusers of Psychiatry* by Lucy Johnstone (1989); Charles Medawar for extracts from *Power and Dependence* and *The Antidepressant Web*; Excerpt from introduction by Irvin Yalom MD to Carl Rogers's *A Way of Being*. Introduction copyright ©1995 by Irvin Yalom. Reprinted by permission of Houghton Mifflin Company. All rights reserved.; Extracts from the *British Medical Journal* with permission from the BMJ Publishing Group; Extracts from the *Diagnostic and Statistical Manual of Mental Disorders, Fourth Edition, Text Revision* reprinted with permission. Copyright ©2000 American Psychiatric Association; *Out of Me* by Fiona Shaw published by Virago. Copyright ©1997 Fiona Shaw; Extract from 'The Tragedy of Schizophrenia' copyright ©Karon/ Widener from *Ethical Human Sciences and Services Journal* used by permission of the Springer Publishing Company, Inc., New York 10012. HarperCollins Publishers Ltd for *My Body, My Enemy* by Claire Beeken (1997); HarperCollins Publishing Ltd for *Toxic Psychiatry* by Dr Peter Breggin (1993); Extract from *The Interpreted World* by Ernesto Spinelli (1989) reprinted by permission of Sage Publications Ltd.

CONTENTS

AUTHOR'S NOTE

No book can act as a substitute for individualised medical or psychological care. The aim of this book is to promote a broader holistic approach to emotional distress, 'mental illness' and suicide. As it can be dangerous to reduce or stop psychiatric medication abruptly, this should only be done with approprate medical guidance and supervision.

ACKNOWLEDGEMENTS

I wish to acknowledge my gratitude to those people whose life stories spurred me on to write this book. I especially want to thank the people who wrote their own stories and those who allowed and encouraged me to write about their life experiences. In most cases (with the exception of Paddy McGowan's) I have changed some minor details to respect their privacy.

I would like to thank Brendan Kennelly for very kindly giving me permission to quote from his poem 'Begin'.

I am deeply grateful for the support of those who believe in the value of this book, particularly Tony Humphreys for his heartfelt and thought-provoking foreword. Thanks to Jim Byrne, senior counsellor at University College, Galway, for his contribution. I would like to thank Jo O'Donoghue, Jane Casey and all at Marino Books for their help and support. Thanks also to Jonathan Williams, literary agent, and Jo O'Donoghue for seeing the possibilities.

It would therefore behove us well – public and politicians alike – to take an active interest in the welfare of our mentally disturbed compatriots, and not to leave their fate to the sole discretion of the experts. They are very far from being expert. And the figures tell us that there's a more than sporting chance that it will be you, or I, or our mother or our brother or our daughter or our spouse who becomes a victim of their ignorance before too long. Medical paternalism can go too far, and we should beware of giving the medical establishment too much legal power.

Dr Donald Gould, *The Black And White Medicine Show, How Doctors Serve and Fail Their Customers*, Hamish Hamilton (1985)

It will generally be found that as soon as the terrors of life reach the point where they outweigh the terrors of death, a man will put an end to his life.

Arthur Schopenhauer

FOREWORD

It was an unfortunate event in history that individuals who were psycho-socially distressed ever came under the umbrella of the medical profession. The assumption was that people so disturbed had some as yet undetected biological disorder, akin to cancer, tuberculosis or heart disease, and that the treatment of choice should be medical. In spite of over 200 years of research, no enduring evidence has emerged to substantiate the medical model of psycho-social distress. Indeed, there is no evidence that conditions such as bipolar depression, schizophrenia, personality disorder, obsessive-compulsive disorder and endogenous depression have any genetic, biochemical, biological or hereditary bases. There is substantial clinical and experimental research evidence that people so labelled have histories that reveal great emotional, social, physical and sexual traumas.

An astonishing aspect of psychiatric care is the tendency to ignore a client's heartrending life history and the total reliance on symptoms for the diagnosis. It is even more intolerable that clients (and their families) are told that their histories have nothing to do with their presenting symptoms.

My own clinical experience is that behaviour always makes sense – hallucinations, illusions, delusions, chronic anxiety, violence, endogenous depression and other such manifestations of inner and outer distress – and that the best intervention is psycho-social in nature and directly responsive to the client's biographical history.

While I have no difficulty in accepting the need at times for short-term psychotropic medication, it is only ethical to point out to clients and their families that such an intervention only reduces symptoms and will do little to resolve the psycho-social causes of the person's distress.

Generally speaking, clinical psychologists and psycho-therapists have tended to reinforce the medical model by being reluctant to take on individuals who have been labelled 'psychotic', while they have readily accepted those termed 'neurotic'. This dual classification of human distress is not even remotely representative of the complexity of people's problems in living, and its only questionable use has been for the prescribing of psycho-tropic drugs. This categorisation needs to be ignored by those psycho-social professions who understand that each client requires a different kind of help.

There are certain characteristics that define the effective psycho-social helper:

- The ability to love their clients unconditionally
- The ability to listen actively with both mind and heart
- The ability to communicate belief in the client's vast potential and giftedness
- The provision of hope so that the person sees the

helper believes that change is possible
- The openness to self-disclosure on their own life's journey
- The communication of understanding so that the client feels secure in revealing his actions and innermost thoughts, feelings, images and dreams
- The provision of safety and support and the calm management of the major suffering that may emerge
- The ability to empathise and show compassion when hurt, rage, guilt or heart-rending sadness rises to the surface

It is encouraging to see in this book that such an approach to human misery is endorsed.

Death rarely comes easily to those who are departing or to those who remain behind. The effects of death by suicide have devastating consequences. Those who remain are often left puzzled or are only too painfully aware of what led the person to take his or her own life. The medical profession – and psychiatry in particular – has not helped in the understanding of suicide by ascribing it to mental illness. There is no research evidence to substantiate this statement. Most of all, a mental illness concept of suicide offers no relief or insight to relatives and friends trying to understand why people choose to take their own lives.

Furthermore, this medical reaction dishonours the person who has committed suicide. Nobody takes their own life lightly. There are always deep, remote and immediate reasons. When clients tell me they have been 'cutting themselves' or 'having thoughts of killing themselves', I let them know that these actions and feelings make sense. To those who cut themselves, I say 'these physical cuts represent the deep emotional cuts you have experienced in life and are crying out to be healed.' To those clients who have feelings that they want to kill themselves I say 'but you are killing time and these thoughts and feelings represent how much of your zest for living has been extinguished and your crying need for someone to see how emotionally near you are to death.'

To respond to suicidal feelings, thoughts or actions with a narrow biological approach (for example, 'these behaviours are the product of a biochemical imbalance') shows no understanding of the complexity of human behaviour and provides no hope to the individual who is deeply troubled. Psychiatry also suggests an existential view of suicide that results in people, particularly parents, being blamed for the person's untimely death. This is grossly inaccurate. Parents and others do not deliberately harm their children, but from their own places of deep insecurity they can subconsciously block their own and their children's emotional and social development.

Attempting to detect and comprehend the causes of suicide is an act of caring for the parents, who often need substantial help themselves. It is also an act of caring for brothers and sisters who are often more at risk following the suicide. The most common illusion – that we all come from happy families – needs to be shattered so that the reality can be faced that there are many adults and children who live lives of quiet (and loud) desperation. There are few families where the parents do not have unresolved emotional baggage from their homes of origin.

The acknowledgement and healing of unresolved conflicts is the only way to reduce the rising rate of suicide. Any profession that subscribes to the illusion of happy families does not help the situation.

This book is a brave attempt to urge not only the medical profession, but all of us, to examine widely and wisely why so many lose their zeal for living and take their precious lives.

Dr Tony Humphreys

INTRODUCTION

Emotional distress is one of the greatest epidemics of our time. As sometimes happens in epidemics, those afflicted are ostracised. Emotions are a fundamental part of the human condition, but in modern society there is little tolerance of the expression of emotion. When friends or loved ones become angry or tearful, we want them to stop because we do not feel comfortable with painful emotions. The greater the distress, the more uncomfortable we feel. We reach the point where we cannot listen any more. We find ways of repackaging emotional distress to make it more palatable. This allows us to distance ourselves from the epidemic.

The main repackaging process we use is to classify emotional distress as 'mental illness'. When I refer to 'mental' or 'psychiatric' illness I use inverted commas, but not with the intention of detracting from the real, often excruciating distress experienced by people who have been so labelled. The inverted commas signify my disquiet at the widespread acceptance of these terms without debate about what the terms mean or what might be better words to use.

People turn to the medical profession for help. GPs deal with 90 per cent of the emotional-distress workload and refer most of the remainder to psychiatrists. The medical profession categorises emotional distress into two groups: the psychiatrically ill and the 'worried well'. Drug treatment is the cornerstone of treatment for those categorised as psychiatrically ill, a label which frequently sticks for life. Emotionally distressed people who doctors decide are not suffering from a 'mental illness' are dismissed as the worried well, needing no treatment. A person's chances of being diagnosed as psychiatrically ill depend on the degree of their emotional distress. Often, neither those labelled as psychiatrically ill nor the worried well receive the help they need from the medical profession, in my opinion.

I present an alternative view of 'mental illness'. Policies regarding the diagnosis and treatment of medical conditions within modern medicine are dominated by the prevailing views of the medical profession. Where 'mental illness' is concerned, the prevailing views within psychiatry dictate how people in emotional distress are dealt with in society. According to most medical experts, 'mental illness' is caused either by a biochemical brain imbalance or a genetic defect. I do not share this view. I believe that the so-called 'mental illnesses' are understandable expressions of emotional pain.

Every year one million people take their own lives worldwide and thirty million people attempt suicide. The prevailing medical belief is that people who end their lives are mentally ill at the time and therefore not in their 'right mind'.

On the contrary, I believe that suicide is the final act of avoidance, which in the context of the person's life always makes sense. We do not need a 'psychiatric illness' explanation for suicide. People who attempt suicide are individuals with unique experiences of life. It is this mosaic of experiences that brings them to the place where suicide seems the only way out of their pain. People who reach the point of suicide all have one thing in common. Overwhelmed by despair, they are desperately trying to put an end to their emotional pain. The tragedy is that in order to do so, they feel they have to kill themselves.

This is not to say that all doctors agree with the prevailing medical views. While my opinions are not shared by the majority of doctors, I am not alone. Some highly respected doctors and psychologists to whom I refer in this book share my concern that the medical approach to emotional distress is misguided. They include Dr Tony Humphreys, a leading Irish psychologist and author; American psychiatrist Dr Peter Breggin, founder of the Centre for the Study of Psychiatry and Psychology in Maryland, USA and author of several books which question modern psychiatry, most notably *Toxic Psychiatry;* experienced British psychologists and authors such as Dorothy Rowe and Lucy Johnstone and the late Dr Bartley Sheehan, coroner and Dublin GP.

What sort of help do we provide for those who fall out of step with the mainstream of society – people who stumble at the hurdles of life and cannot pick themselves up, people whose hopes and dreams have been dashed, those who are labelled by society as different, those who are consumed by insecurity and self-doubt? These are people who have been hurt so often they cannot take any more: men and women in relationships that initially carried such hopes but which have, over the years, lost their lustre, and those who have experienced far more fear and hurt in their lives than love. They are consumed with loneliness but are afraid to show it: they are human beings like you and me.

Some people become so despairing that they take their own lives. Many turn to the medical system for help, only to end up diagnosed as suffering from a 'mental illness', or told that there is nothing wrong with them. The escalating suicide rate is a wake-up call to us all. Concluding that suicide is the result of 'mental illness' may make us feel better, but it is passing the buck. People take their own lives when they reach the point of no hope.

Over the past twenty years, most countries have witnessed their suicide rates increase dramatically. For every suicide, at least twenty people attempt suicide. Ireland has one of the fastest-growing suicide rates in the world – there were 413 suicides in Ireland in 2000. More than four thousand people take their own lives in Britain each year – one suicide every seventy minutes. In Britain and Ireland, the increasing suicide rate has been particularly noticeable among young men. The suicide rate in young men under 35 has doubled in Britain over the past twenty years, and the increase in this group has been even more dramatic in Ireland. Suicide in men between 15 and 35 years of age is now up there with road traffic accidents as one of the most common causes of death in that age group. Although reducing the suicide rate in Britain by 15 per cent has been a stated national priority of the British Department of Health since 1992, the British suicide rates keep rising. In 1998 the US Surgeon General stated that it was high time Americans had an honest debate on mental health. I believe such a debate is as necessary in Europe as in America.

1
—

MEDICAL RESEARCH

During my early years as a medical doctor, I unquestioningly believed that medical research was beyond reproach, the foundation upon which trustworthy scientific medical practice was built. Eighteen years later, my views have changed considerably. The calibre of medical research affects the quality of medical care. It therefore seems appropriate at the outset to explore the reliability of medical research.

The results of medical research are rarely questioned. People presume that because medical research is scientific, it must be reliable. This perception of medical research is regularly reinforced by doctors in the media. For instance, psychiatrist Dr Matthew Hotopf, a lecturer at the Institute of Psychiatry at London's Maudsley Hospital, explained in the *Guardian* of 7 April 1998 why doctors are sceptical of alternative medicine. He said that all medical treatments have to be carefully evaluated using randomised trials. The implicit assumption in comments such as Dr Hotopf's is that everything doctors do has been researched thoroughly and to a very high standard. Unfortunately, this is not always the case.

According to two scientists who have been auditing trials of new medicines for the past ten years, some clinical trials are so badly flawed that they endanger the health of the patients who take part in them. On 27 July 1999 the *Guardian* reported that scientists Wendy Boh-aychuk and Graham Ball were appalled at the poor standards they have consistently found in clinical trials of new drugs. In a third of the trials they reviewed, they found significant under-reporting of side effects. Dr Ball said that the government had no idea what was going on.

Dr Stephen Penford Lock is a former editor of the prestigious *British Medical Journal.* In an interview with journalist Maresa Fagan, published in the *Irish Medical Times* of 15 October 1999, Dr Penford Lock stated that between 10 and 30 per cent of medical research is known to be fraudulent, involving plagiarism and the invention of data. He said that no system existed to deal with suspected cases of fraudulent research. He expressed his concern that large drug trials were often not replicated and could be influenced by pharmaceutical companies. He added that money could act as an incentive, with some trials receiving over £1,000 per patient. He also pointed out that some researchers invented data, having con-vinced themselves of their findings before they had actually obtained results.

In the *British Medical Journal* of 5 October 1991, editor Richard Smith discussed a presentation given the previous week in Manchester by Dr David Eddy, then professor of Health Policy and Management at Duke University, North Carolina. Dr Eddy told the conference:

Only about 15 per cent of medical interventions are supported by solid scientific evidence. This is partly because only 1 per cent of articles in medical journals are scientifically sound, and partly because many treatments have never been assessed at all. Confident statements in textbooks and medical journals regarding medical treatments have simply been handed down from generation to generation, without having been scientifically assessed.

In *Medicine Weekly* on 24 September 1997, Irish psychiatrist Dr Peadar O'Grady expressed his concerns about medical research:

Most medical research is unhelpfully biased, or incompetently or fraudulently constructed, sometimes all of the above. Research is largely funded by pharmaceutical companies, which obviously favour research that will either develop a new drug, or show an old drug to be better than other therapies. Of the research that is done, drug research has an unfair advantage in that advertising from drug companies is what most journals almost entirely run on. Refusing a piece of [drug] research might endanger such revenue, and to publish research showing a drug to be dangerous, useless or less effective than alternatives could be positively suicidal for a journal. The editor of a journal of psychological research once told me that research was biased by funding both of the research itself and of the journals in which it is published.

Even in esteemed journals such as the *British Journal of Psychiatry*, it has been estimated that statistical errors occur in 40 per cent of published research, casting serious doubt on the conclusions drawn from these studies. In my opinion, medical research into emotional distress and 'mental illness' should be broadly based along the following lines:

THE PROBLEM	POSSIBLE CAUSES AND TREATMENTS	FOCUS OF MEDICAL RESEARCH
'mental illness'	physical emotional psychological spiritual social relationships others	Research all theories without bias in the search for the cause and the appropriate treatment

The approach of some scientists would appear to be significantly more narrow:

THE PROBLEM	POSSIBLE CAUSES AND TREATMENTS	FOCUS OF MEDICAL RESEARCH
'mental illness'	physical or biological (genetic or biochemical)	Research directed at proving the cause and treatment of mental illness is physical/biological

Occasionally medical research is carried out which looks beyond this narrow focus. Dr Margo Wrigley is a consultant psychiatrist at the Mater Hospital, Dublin. Dr Wrigley assessed the value of 'pet therapy' in patients with dementia. According to Dr Wrigley, the study revealed a statistically significant decrease in abnormal behaviour and an increase in social behaviour when dogs were present in the most disturbed groups. Dementia is characterised by brain-cell degeneration, yet pets managed to connect with patients suffering from dementia. Having a dog around benefited patients with severe dementia. But research such as this does not sit well with the medical belief that 'mental illnesses' are physical illnesses requiring physical treatments. Dr Wrigley's research raises the possibility that non-drug treatments which provide love and companionship may considerably benefit patients. In my experience, research which goes against the medical grain slips quietly into obscurity. I do not anticipate a rush within psychiatry to investigate 'pet therapy' much further.

Most medical research is now funded by pharmaceutical companies, a fact which clearly influences what type of medical research is carried out. Usually when drug companies 'donate' money for medical research, only biomedical research will be funded by this investment. Biomedical research concentrates on the body as a physical entity and on finding drug treatments as cures for illnesses. Pharmaceutical companies are entitled to promote their own industry. But little funding is available for research into the emotional, psychological and relationship aspects of 'mental illness'.

Most medical researchers strive to be objective but there are subtle factors that contribute a strong subjective flavour to medical research. In modern psychiatry there is a broad consensus that 'mental illnesses' are caused by biochemical or genetic defects. This strongly held core belief influences how medical researchers carry out and interpret their research. Dr Ernesto Spinelli is a highly regarded British psychotherapist, author and principal lecturer at the School of Psychotherapy and Counselling, Regent's College. In his book *The Interpreted World* he considers the objectivity of research, cautioning that the assumed objectivity between the data being analysed and the person who analyses the data is questionable given that every person – including researchers – continuously interprets the world through the lens of previous ex-periences, presumptions and expectations.

Modern psychiatry's idea of Utopia would be where every psychological symptom was proven to be caused by a biochemical imbalance, a genetic effect or some other bodily cause, treatable with drugs, genetic substitution or other medically attractive means. Psychiatry draws conclusions, creates research and constructs treatment plans which aspire to this Utopia and which are often not backed up by solid scientific practice. Aspiring as they do to be scientific, doctors would do well to remember that the first pre-requisite of any true scientist is an open mind. As Dr David Marshall wrote in October 1998 in *Medicine Weekly*, rarely do researchers' conclusions differ significantly from their previously held opinions.

Consensus views are often presented to the public as confirmation that psychiatry's beliefs are correct and its practices the best available. There is safety in numbers. But consensus views are merely a reflection of the prevailing views of the group which hold them. Consensus views do not always get it right. The medical treatment of depression, schizophrenia and other 'psychiatric illnesses' is based on consensus views rather than scientific proof.

Misinterpretations and omissions regarding medical research can originate from the researchers themselves, from other doctors interpreting the research, or from journalists attempting to interpret doctors and medical research. What follows is, in my opinion, an example of serious misinterpretation of medical research.

In the *Irish Examiner* newspaper of 13 May 1999, leading psychiatrist Patricia Casey, professor of psychiatry at University College, Dublin, was quoted as saying that counselling is a waste of time for treating depression. Journalist Caroline O'Doherty wrote that Professor Casey was speaking following the publication of a study in the prestigious *British Medical Journal* which showed that counselling had no benefits for patients with depression. This surprised me, since I have encountered many people with depression who derived considerable benefit from counselling. (For example, at the launch of Cork Advocacy Network in January 2001, the organisers expected two to three hundred people to attend. Over six hundred people attended, a testament to public disquiet about psychiatric care. This organisation aims to provide people diagnosed as having 'mental illness' with a voice and support. Speaker after speaker described traumatic experiences at the hands of psychiatry. Many people attributed their recovery to social support and counselling rather than to the psychiatric services.)

I decided to investigate for myself. I phoned Professor Casey's secretary and obtained details of that *British Medical Journal* article, which turned out to be a study on depression by Professor U. Malt of the University of Oslo, published in the *British Medical Journal* of 1 May 1999. The only 'counselling' involved in this study was that GPs were asked to be supportive to their patients during the consultation. But since counselling is understood to be carried out by a trained therapist, and since few GPs have any training in counselling, surely supportive words from the GP do not constitute counselling. Indeed, the research paper clearly stated that specific forms of counselling were excluded from the study.

I believe that this inaccuracy was carried further by Professor Casey in an article she wrote for the *Sunday Business Post* of 4 July 1999 with the interesting title 'Counsellor, Heal Thyself'. In that article, Professor Casey wrote that Professor Malt's study demonstrated that counselling was significantly less effective in the treatment of depressive illness than antidepressants. She did not specifically mention Malt's name, but at my request Professor Casey's secretary confirmed with her that it was Malt's study to which she referred.

In my opinion, people reading those newspaper articles involving a highly influential psychiatrist would erroneously conclude that medical experts had now established the superiority of antidepressants over counselling in the treatment of depression. Since true counselling was not allowed in this study, such conclusions seem grossly inaccurate.

A week later, Dr Ivor Browne – Professor Casey's predecessor as professor of psychiatry at University College, Dublin – challenged her interpretation of that research study. In the *Sunday Business Post* of 11 July 1999, Dr Browne wrote that the reference to counselling in Professor Malt's study was merely incidental. The central concern of that paper was a comparison of one antidepressant drug with another. Dr Browne pointed out that:

> this study did not involve any significant psychotherapy or counselling input. I can only assume that Professor Casey was pressed for time when she read this.

I believe that many such misinterpretations of medical research reach the public domain through the medical profession. Consequently, incorrect information is given to the public, who draw incorrect conclusions. Rarely is the record subsequently set straight. It is most unusual that one professor should so openly challenge another in the national newspapers. The depth of Dr Browne's concern is encapsulated in his sentence: 'Could it be that orthodox psychiatry has let so many people down?' Coming from an experienced and highly respected psychiatrist, well known for his human compassion, these are strong words indeed. Dr Browne wrote that there is a well-established body of research demonstrating the effectiveness of counselling and psychotherapy, and he expressed surprise that Professor Casey seemed to be unaware of these studies.

In my opinion, Professor Malt's depression study raised more questions than answers. For example, Professor Malt found that almost half of the study participants who were put on placebo (inert sugar-pills) recovered from their depression in the course of the six-month trial. They were not on any medication, yet their depression lifted. There was not a marked difference between the effectiveness of the sugar pills and the antidepressant drugs used in the trial. Remission occurred in 47 per cent of patients who received the placebo, compared to 54 per cent with one antidepressant and 61 per cent for a second antidepressant.

In this depression study, Professor Malt did point out a basic flaw in the vast majority of medical research into the treatment of depression and other 'mental illnesses'. Depression-research trials typically assess patients for five to six weeks – not nearly long enough to come to meaningful conclusions. The way in which research projects are structured can distort their objectivity. In the above study, patients who had previously failed to respond to antidepressant drugs – including the two antidepressants tested in this study – were excluded from the study. So were patients who had severe depression, and those whose depression had lasted for more than one year. Had these groups of patients been included in this trial, the antidepressants would have been likely to be even less effective. How can research be truly representative of the whole population when several important groups are excluded from the research?

In many studies, a separate mini-trial – known as a 'placebo run-in' – precedes the actual clinical trial, to identify people likely to respond well to the placebo against which the drug on trial will be tested. People who respond well to the placebo are then excluded from the trial. This has serious implications. The trial can no longer be considered to be a broadly based, scientific trial, since one specific group has been excluded. An artificially streamlined pool of people is entered into the trial, which is no longer representative of the broad variety of people who attend doctors every day seeking help. How can the effectiveness of a placebo be properly tested when the study sets out to exclude people who respond well to it? I have never heard of the placebo run-in's corollary – a drug run-in study – being carried out, to remove from studies people who respond exceptionally well to the drug being tested. In 1972, medical researcher L. E. Hollister described his experiences of a placebo run-in trial. All depressed patients who entered the hospital and were candidates for the study were initially placed on a placebo for one week. At the end of the week, 50 per cent of these patients had improved so much that they could no longer be defined as depressed, so they had to be withdrawn from the trial. Preoccupied with proving that antidepressants work, the medical profession has avoided explaining why so many depressed people get better with placebos alone.

Placebo run-in trials have the effect of making the placebo look less effective than it would otherwise be. For example, Professor Malt did not use a placebo run-in prior to his study and the effectiveness of placebo was 46 per cent. This compares to around 30 per cent in studies involving placebo run-ins. And of course, any strategy which reduces the apparent effect of a placebo enhances and possibly exaggerates the effect of the drug being tested.

Because most medical research into suicide concentrates on finding a biochemical imbalance as the cause, other possible contributing factors to suicide do not receive the attention they deserve. Many psychiatrists believe that an imbalance of one brain chemical in particular – serotonin – may be the underlying cause of suicide, just as an imbalance of this same chemical is purported to be the cause of depression.

In *Medicine Weekly* of 17 December 1997, Professor Patricia Casey wrote an article with the title 'Prozac Is Now the Scapegoat of the Ignorant and the Cruel'. I found that title interesting because, in my opinion, if one has conscientiously held concerns about the current prescribing of Prozac and other antidepressants, it does not automatically mean that one is either ignorant or cruel. In the article, Professor Casey wrote that depression is a 'debilitative biological disorder', that 'depressive illness is organic in nature', and referred to depression as 'biological depression'.

I felt from this article that Professor Casey seemed convinced that depression is an organic, biological illness. But as I understand it, a biological or organic cause for depression has never been proven. Certainly there are theories suggesting this, but I was not aware that any of these theories had been proven to be true. I therefore wrote the following letter to that journal:

Dear Editor

I refer to Professor Casey's article on Prozac in your December 17 edition. On three occasions in this article, Professor Casey refers to the view that depression is biological in nature. I would be very grateful if, through the pages of your journal, Professor Casey would outline the research (with references) which proves conclusively that the cause of depression is biological or biochemical.

Professor Casey's reply in *Medicine Weekly* on 14 January 1998 was brief:

In his letter of 14 January, Dr Terry Lynch requests that I provide references to substantiate my statements relating to the biological nature of depressive illness. I suggest that he purchase any of the postgraduate textbooks of psychiatry, where he will find a myriad of references to same.

Far from satisfied with this short reply, I wrote the following letter in response, which was published in the 4 February 1998 edition of *Medicine Weekly.*

Dear Editor

I refer to Professor Patricia Casey's reply to my letter of 14 January in which I requested Professor Casey to outline, with references, whatever conclusive proof there is (if any exists) that the cause of depression is biological. Rather than telling me to go off and buy some psychiatry books, I had hoped that Professor Casey would answer my question.

I am well aware that there are many references in psychiatry books to the view that depression is biological in origin. However, I have not yet come across any article in any journal which constitutes conclusive proof that the cause of depression is biological.

Many articles and much research have linked depression with biochemical changes in the brain. But these are not in themselves proof of a biochemical or biological cause for depression. While these biological changes could point towards a biochemical cause for depression, they could equally be the effect of the depressive state.

What is the current position? Do we have conclusive proof that the cause of depression is biological? If so, then I would love to hear precisely what that proof is. If we do not at this time have conclusive proof that the cause of depression is biological, then our belief in the biological causation of depression is not proven fact; rather it is a working hypothesis. The thing about a hypothesis is that while it may well be right, it may also be wrong. Which is it? Proven fact, or working hypothesis?

I believe that the question I was asking is profoundly important. Yet neither Professor Casey nor any other doctor replied to my second letter. I rang the journal to make sure that Professor Casey had received my second letter, and the editor assured me that she had.

There was no further correspondence or discussion on this issue. Every two weeks, 6,500 copies of this journal are printed. The journal is sent to virtually every doctor in Ireland, including every GP and psychiatrist in the country. Yet not one doctor wrote to the journal to address the serious issue I had raised. I felt that there was a reluctance within psychiatry (and medicine in general) to discuss what is a fundamentally important question – what causes depression?

I felt vindicated a year later when Professor Casey wrote (in an article on the new treatments of depression in the *Irish Medical News* of 22 February 1999) that the exact biochemical underpinnings of mood disorders were not known. And according to British professor of psychiatry Dr C. Thompson, writing in *Medical Dialogue* in December 1997, the biological basis of depression has been a hypothesis for more than thirty years.

Although any association between serotonin and depression and suicide is purely speculative, medical experts frequently describe this link with great conviction. As a consequence, journalists unwittingly propagate the misinformation, basing their writings on the statements of the experts. Mary Kenny is an experienced journalist. In December 1998 in the *Irish Independent* she wrote:

> Serotonin is the natural chemical which produces the unmistakable feel-good factor; when you are happy, your serotonin is high. And

> when you are wretched, your serotonin is low. An unhappy event in your life sends your serotonin level shooting right down. Prozac was developed as a consequence of the discovery of serotonin levels. Prozac makes people feel good by upping their serotonin levels.

Mary Kenny's comments seem reasonable. Unfortunately, not one of these statements is factually correct. Serotonin has not been proven to produce a feel-good factor. No link has been established between happiness and high serotonin levels, nor between unhappiness and low serotonin levels. No evidence exists that unhappy events send serotonin levels 'shooting down'. It is far from established that Prozac makes people feel good by 'upping their serotonin levels', despite all the propaganda.

Mary Kenny can be forgiven for not knowing this, given how freely doctors speak of theories as if they were established facts. Thus, millions of people come to accept as fact something which is no more than a theory. I believe the medical profession has a responsibility to ensure that the public are not misinformed.

References to biochemical abnormalities occur regularly in the media. In an article in the *Irish Examiner* on 14 August 2000 on the over-prescription of antidepression drugs, journalist Linda McGrory wrote that Prozac and similar antidepressant drugs 'restore levels of the neurotransmitter serotonin in the brain'. While it is worrying that a journalist would express something so inaccurate as this, it is alarming when a medical doctor does so. In this article, Dr Robert Daly, professor of psychiatry at University College Cork, was

quoted as saying that antidepressants target a brain biochemical deficiency.

Meanwhile, as the medical profession searches for a
physical cause of 'mental illness' and suicide, the real
issues are calling for attention. The social, emotional,
psychological and relationship issues which are usually more
than enough to explain why people become 'mentally ill' and
why people take their lives are overlooked by modern
medicine. Biochemical brain defects may occur; we simply
do not know whether they do or not. In my opinion, the
best approach in carrying out research is to keep an open
mind, and to research all possible causes with equal
enthusiasm. This is not happening at the moment.

I believe that the medical profession's bias towards
biological and genetic research as opposed to emotional
and psychological research was well demonstrated in an
article in the *Irish Medical Times* of 31 March 2000 by
psychiatrist Dr Aiveen Kirley. Dr Kirley wrote that there
is currently a debate within medicine on the question of
whether or not depression and anxiety are separate
entities from genetic, neurobiological and pharmaco-
logical standpoints. She did not mention emotional, social
or psychological standpoints, and devoted little space to
exploring the latter three. Under the heading 'Treatment',
Dr Kirley explored the various medication options in great
detail. In contrast, psychotherapy and relaxation tech-
niques were briefly discussed in her final paragraph,
receiving roughly one-twentieth of the attention given to
drug treatments.

Even if it were demonstrated that people with depression or those who take their own life did have an

imbalance of serotonin or some other brain chemical, the obvious question – which seems to have escaped the medical profession – remains. Is the brain chemical imbalance the cause of the depression or the suicide, or is the imbalance produced by the long-standing emotional and psychological distress that person has endured, often for many years?

Because psychiatrists are now seen as the experts on suicide, the majority of research into 'mental illness' and suicide is dominated by psychiatry and its beliefs. Those who believe that psychiatry's approach is seriously misguided have been sidelined.

Dr James McCormack, Professor Emeritus at the department of community health and general practice at Trinity College, Dublin, is known for his scepticism regarding many modern medical treatments. In an interview in the *Examiner* on 8 October 1999, Dr McCormack said that antibiotics, tonics, cough bottles and tranquillizers were the present-day placebos. I believe that antidepressants, regularly offered by doctors to patients at the first hint of emotional distress, should be added to this list.

Medical research is carried out by human beings, not machines. Researchers too have their hopes and their dreams, their prejudices and their biases, their career ambitions, their fallibility. Consequently I believe the public should be cautious about taking the findings of medical research at face value, including medical research into 'mental illness' and suicide.

2

DOES 'MENTAL ILLNESS' EXIST?

Approximately 25 per cent of the population suffer from a so-called 'psychiatric illness'. Up to 10 per cent suffer from depression and one per cent from schizophrenia. The remainder suffer from conditions such as manic depression, anxiety, eating disorders, and addiction to drugs and alcohol.

A central feature of 'mental illness' is that the sufferer exhibits features and behaviour deemed by both the medical profession and the public to be abnormal. In depression, the abnormal features include the depth of the depression, self-hatred and weight loss. With schizophrenia, there are hallucinations, delusions, complex thought-patterns and withdrawal from life.

Extremes of elation and depression are characteristic of manic depression. Anxiety is considered a psychiatric illness when it is severe enough to disrupt a person's life. The abnormal feature in eating disorders is erratic behaviour around food. In anorexia, people starve themselves for days or weeks on end, often losing so much weight that their lives are in danger. Bulimia sufferers control their intake of food obsessively and can go on frenzied food binges, stuffing themselves with more food than most people would eat in a week. In the case of addiction to drugs and alcohol, the abnormal behaviours include the extreme desire for the substance and the person's reactions having taken the substance. According to the prevailing medical view, because these behaviours are so unusual, they should be defined as 'mental illnesses'. These 'illnesses', the theory goes, are most likely caused by a physical bodily defect: either a bio-chemical imbalance in the brain or a genetic defect. Medical treatment for these conditions is built around these beliefs. Antidepressant drugs are advised for depression. Tranquil-lizers are widely prescribed for anxiety. Schizophrenia is treated with major tranquillizers. The treatment of choice for manic depression is lithium. Antidepressants are recommended for eating disorders.

GPs diagnose and treat 90 per cent of 'mental illness' patients. They refer most of the remainder to psych-iatrists. Psychiatry is seen as the specialty with the greatest expertise in emotional distress and 'psychiatric illness'. The views of those who do not always concur with psychiatry such as psychologists, counsellors and psycho-therapists are dismissed by the medical profession as well-meaning but misguided. But cracks appear when the prevailing medical view of 'psychiatric illness' is exam-ined.

Take the medical treatment of 'psychiatric illness'. No specific medical cure exists for any psychiatric condition. The best that medical treatment can offer is a suppression of symptoms. Major tranquillizer drugs used in the treatment of schizophrenia and manic depression are

blunt instruments, numbing the person's thought processes. Tranquillizers used to treat anxiety are also blunt
instruments. They sedate, resulting in a temporary
reduction of anxiety – but at a price. People become
immune to these tranquillizers within a few weeks. Higher
doses are then taken, but their effectiveness quickly
wanes. In addition to the anxiety, the person may now
have a second problem: addiction to the 'treatment'
prescribed by the doctor.

While lithium has been hailed as a very effective
treatment for manic depression, doctors do not know how
lithium works. Like other psychiatric treatments, lithium
appears to numb the brain's ability to function. Relatives
of those diagnosed with manic depression understandably
live in fear of patients ceasing to take their lithium. While
the numbing effect of lithium on the brain does reduce
the swings of elation and depression, making life easier
for those around the patient, many people taking lithium
hate this drug. They feel sedated. They cannot think
clearly; they feel as if parts of their brain have been
switched off.

The psychiatric approach to 'mental illness' is not
unanimously accepted within the caring professions. Dr
Peter Breggin has been an outspoken critic of psychiatry
throughout his career. He has written extensively about
the dangers of psychiatry. Dr Breggin maintains that
antidepressant drugs have never been shown to reduce
the suicide rate. Indeed, some studies have suggested an
increased suicide rate in those prescribed antidepressant
drugs. According to Dr Breggin, the threat of being locked
away in a mental institution against their will scares many

suicidal people away from seeking help when they are in distress. In *Toxic Psychiatry* Dr Breggin wrote:

> Why psychiatrists themselves would favour biochemical and genetic theories is no secret. Their entire professional identity depends on this ideology, and in the case of researchers, their funding can be totally dependent on it.

Within psychiatry and modern medicine, Dr Breggin is not a popular man. His many books and public statements about the dangers of psychiatry and the need for safer and more humane treatments receive little attention within the medical profession. Why? Because he is rocking the medical boat. He is a threat to the status and position of his psychiatric colleagues. He is questioning that upon which the entire industry of psychiatry depends – the very existence of 'mental illness'.

Dorothy Rowe is an experienced and outspoken clinical psychologist and the author of ten bestselling books on psychology. She has lived and worked in Britain for the past thirty years. In the foreword to Dr Breggin's *Toxic Psychiatry*, she outlines why she thought psychiatrists insist on the existence of 'mental illness':

> If such illnesses exist, then they can be treated by one profession only – psychiatry. But if such illnesses do not exist, if 'illness' is simply a metaphor for the various ways we can feel despair, fear and alienation, then psychiatrists have nothing unique to offer. Anyone who has

the necessary wisdom, sympathy and patience – a psychologist, a counsellor, a good friend – could give the help the sufferer needs. Psychiatry would vanish, just as the profession of hangman vanished from Britain once the death penalty was abolished.

While doctors repeatedly state that biochemical imbalances cause psychiatric illnesses, their behaviour does not support this view. When doctors suspect that a person has a biochemical imbalance, they will carry out the appropriate test to check this out. They will compare the test results to well-established guidelines, and decide whether or not the person has a biochemical imbalance. For example, diabetes is diagnosed when the blood sugar level is raised, and thyroid disease is diagnosed when the blood thyroid hormone level is either reduced or excessive. No doctor would dream of presuming that a person had either diabetes or thyroid disease without first carrying out the appropriate blood test. Over time, this blood test is regularly repeated to assess the patient's condition. The treatment dosage is dictated largely by the results of the ongoing blood-test results.

However, doctors approach 'mental illness' very differently. In twenty years of working as a doctor, I have never heard of any person having a diagnosis of depression, schizophrenia, manic depression or any other psychiatric condition confirmed by a blood test, or any other test. Dosages of psychiatric drugs are not adjusted according to blood-test results, as happens with all biochemically based illnesses. When doctors decide to stop treatment in cases of 'mental illness', no blood test is done to confirm that the supposed biochemical abnormality has been eradicated. This would not happen with any known biochemical abnormality. Why no tests? Because no such tests exist – because no biochemical abnormality has been demonstrated in any psychiatric illness. Does this not raise serious questions about the medical profession's claims that psychiatric illnesses are caused by biochemical abnormalities in the brain? Manic depression is the only psychiatric condition where regular blood tests are carried out. These tests are not done to check the level of any body chemical. Rather, they are done to check the blood levels of the treatment drug lithium, a drug with highly toxic side effects.

Similarly, when doctors suspect the presence of a known genetic illness, they will typically confirm the diagnosis with genetic tests. No such tests are ever carried out to confirm a diagnosis of depression, manic depression, schizophrenia, or any other 'mental illness'. Whether such confirmatory tests for 'mental illness' will become possible in the future is purely speculative. Right now, no genetic tests are carried out on 'mentally ill' patients because no genetic cause has been established and no such tests exist for 'mental illness'.

If brain chemical changes occur during our daily mental activities, these changes are likely to be extremely fast-moving and complex, just as our thoughts and feelings are. The truth is that medical science has little understanding of the extremely complex and delicate brain chemical interactions which occur hundreds of times per second every day of our lives.

Irish psychologist and author Dr Tony Humphreys has for years been a critic of psychiatry and modern medicine's approach to emotional distress. On many occasions I have heard Dr Humphreys say that the experiences of his clients over many years indicate to him that psychiatry has long outlived its usefulness. He maintains that the medical approach to so-called 'mental illness' is seriously misguided. Dr Humphreys believes that, rather than dismissing symptoms as meaningless, as evidence of 'mental illness' and suppressing them with psychiatric drugs, these symptoms should be made sense of in the overall context of the person's life. He believes that people who experience mental suffering need human understanding and support rather than psychiatric drugs.

Dr Donal Gould is a former professor of physiology and senior medical lecturer at St Bartholemew's Hospital, London. In his book *The Black and White Medicine Show* he wrote:

> Psychiatry, far from being an exact science, hardly merits description as a scientific discipline at all. We still have small idea of the mechanism of intellectual disorders and deficiencies, and such insights as have been gained within recent years are largely the result of neurophysiologists and other laboratory-based investigators rather than the results of the observations and the acumen of clinical psychiatrists. Good psychiatrists are good not because they know what is actually happening in the computer circuits of the mind, and how the nerve cells work, and what is amiss in the brain

cells of the mentally ill. They are good because they are humane, intelligent, empathic, priest-like men and women who understand the problems of their fellow human beings in distress, and so can give the support and encouragement their patients need. Most of the 'special' insights they possess are to be found in the Bible and in the works of Shakespeare. Bad psychiatrists are bad because, while sharing their superior colleagues' ignorance of the brain's machinery, they lack their human virtues and intelligence and common sense, and in the absence of a teachable body of proven psychiatric wisdom, they are left without the resources needed for the successful performance of an exceptionally demanding branch of medical practice.

If modern medicine's main interest really was the welfare of its patients rather than its own survival, position and status, doctors would listen to their critics very carefully. They would look seriously at their own beliefs and practices. They would invite those who question the conventional view to meet with modern medicine in a joint and holistic effort to improve the quality of care available to the general public. But this is not happening. On the contrary, in my opinion most mainstream psychiatrists display little interest in developing such a holistic model of mental health.

Both psychiatry and psychology could potentially claim expertise in emotional distress, 'psychiatric illness' and suicide. Each group has its own view about the cause, treatment, research, and other aspects of 'mental illness'. On many issues, there is a vast difference between the views of each group, increasing the likelihood that one would seek to dominate the other. Here is a brief summary of the philosophy and beliefs of each group:

Psychiatry

The perception of psychiatrists as kindly old gentlemen who listen with great compassion and understanding is rapidly dying out. Modern psychiatrists are more likely to see themselves as scientists. Their attention is on forming a diagnosis rather than exploring feelings and issues with their patients.

Most psychiatrists believe that the cause of mental illness is primarily physical: either a biochemical abnormality in the brain or a genetic defect. The practice of modern psychiatry revolves around this unproven theory. There is a strong alliance between psychiatry and the pharmaceutical industry. Drug companies have a vested interest in promoting psychiatry rather than psychology. The predominant theory of psychiatry is attractive to the pharmaceutical industry: biochemical brain abnormalities can – in theory – be corrected by drugs; genetic defects can – again, in theory – be corrected by genetic substitution. Either way, there is money in it for the pharmaceutical industry.

Psychology, Psychotherapy and Counselling

While there are differing views within these professions, a predominant belief within psychology, psychotherapy and counselling is that the cause of 'mental illness' lies in emotional, psychological, social and relationship conflicts. They believe that treatment should primarily focus on emotional and psychological issues. Psychotherapy and counselling are broad terms to describe the treatments used by psychologists, psychotherapists and counsellors.

In the earlier part of the twentieth century, psychiatry was something of a Cinderella. During the past fifty years, it has managed to become increasingly accepted, within the medical profession and the general public. Psychiatry has achieved this respectability by developing itself along the lines of other medical specialties, aspiring to become increasingly scientific.

Filled with a passionate desire to establish psychiatry as a scientific, respectable branch of medicine, the pioneering psychiatrists of fifty years ago made an error of judgement. They first arrived at their conclusion, and subsequently set up their research to prove that their conclusion was the correct one. Deciding that 'mental illness' was caused by a physical brain defect rather than emotional distress, they designed their research to establish that this was the case. The cart came before the horse.

These zealous doctors needed financial backing to carry out and publish their research. Enter the emerging pharmaceutical industry, which saw the magnitude of their opportunity and took it well. Drug companies began financing medical research and medical journals. Before long, the medical profession – psychiatry included – became enormously financially dependent on the pharmaceutical industry.

Through this funding the pharmaceutical companies subtly increased their control over what type of research was carried out. Indeed, the pharmaceutical industry has shaped the direction of modern medicine much more than is generally realised. He who pays the piper usually gets to call the tune.

The history of psychiatry is far from inspiring. Contrary to the general perception, modern medicine's handling of emotional distress during the past one hundred years is filled with a succession of dangerous, addictive 'treatments'. Most of these 'treatments' were discarded twenty to thirty years after they were first introduced. They were replaced with newer and 'safer' treatments which themselves were subsequently found to be either dangerous, ineffective or addictive. This pattern continues today.

Charles Medawar works with Social Audit UK, the publishing arm of Public Interest Research Centre Ltd, a UK registered charity. The remit of this centre is to assess the quality and value of public services, including health care. He has carried out extensive research on tranquillizers and antidepressants. According to Medawar, in an article entitled 'Antidepressants – Hooked on the Happy Drug' in the February 1998 edition of *What Doctors Don't Tell You*:

> Over the past 200 years, doctors have prescribed an almost uninterrupted succession of addictive drugs, always in the belief that they would not cause dependence or that patients would be mainly responsible if they did. From alcohol and opium to barbiturates and benzodiazepine

tranquillizers [such as diazepam, Valium, Ativan, Xanax, Tranxene] and all other tranquillizers and sleeping tablets currently prescribed by doctors, all of these drugs have been prescribed as sedatives for mental distress.

In his book *Power and Dependence* Medawar wrote:

The evidence suggests that the providers of medicine [doctors] keep making the same mistakes, mainly because they have been allowed to deny how badly things have gone wrong. Virtually every anti-anxiety drug and sleeping pill ever prescribed has proved to be a drug of dependence – yet each one has been prescribed, often for many years, as if the risk did not exist. This pattern of error has been established over the past 100 years or more, and continues to this day.

Alcohol, morphine, heroin, cocaine, amphetamines, barbiturates, sleeping tablets and tranquillizers were each, in their day, introduced as wonderful and non-addictive treatments. The addictiveness of each of these drugs went unnoticed for decades after they were introduced. In the case of each of these drugs, the medical profession has been slow to accept their addictive potential. With many, the push to have them recognised as addictive came, not from within the medical profession, but from the public. People had great difficulty in convincing the medical profession that these drugs were addictive. Throughout history, millions of drug addicts have been created by the 'best' modern medical treatments of the day.

Therefore, when doctors say that antidepressant drugs are not addictive, remember that they said precisely the same thing about a long list of addictive 'treatments'. Contrary to what you hear from psychiatrists, there is evidence to suggest that the newer antidepressants such as Prozac, Seroxat, Faverin and others may well be addictive. These drugs give an energy buzz, often making people feel better. But so did amphetamines and bar-biturates, which were subsequently – many years and millions of patients later – found to be a very addictive group of drugs. I know many people who have had great difficulty in coming off these newer antidepressant drugs.

I believe that doctors, faced with patients who are getting withdrawal symptoms from Seroxat, Prozac or other newer antidepressants, incorrectly conclude that the underlying depression is not yet healed and the drug prescription is renewed. Doctors made this error of judgement in the past in the case of tranquillizers and other addictive drugs. In my opinion, there is a distinct possibility that in twenty years' time the addictive potent-ial of the newer antidepressants may be confirmed. By then, the medical profession will have newer drugs to prescribe, which, of course, will not be at all addictive. This pattern will continue until the expertise and method-ology of the medical profession receives a thorough and independent investigation.

Most of the other treatments used by modern medicine in the control of so-called 'mental illness' during the past fifty years have been found to be either dangerous or useless or both. A zealous enthusiasm, a strong desire to help one's fellow man and a deep conviction that you are right can have disastrous consequences. The combination of enthusiasm, desire and conviction when combined can deprive a person of the priceless quality of objectivity: the ability to see the wood for the trees. For example, a central belief of many of the religions who have been involved in religious conflicts down through the centuries is 'thou shalt not kill'. Yet throughout history, more people have been murdered in conflicts about religion than for any other single cause.

Similarly, in medicine, enthusiasm, desire and conviction are no guarantee that no harm will result from the actions of highly motivated doctors. Here are some of the 'treatments' which medical experts fervently believed in as recently as twenty years ago. These treatments caused many problems, including numerous fatalities.

Lobotomy

A lobotomy is a surgical procedure during which part of the brain (usually the frontal lobes) is cut. That part of the brain ceases to function. This barbaric procedure was used as recently as twenty to thirty years ago for a wide variety of psychological and emotional problems. It is still used occasionally. Countless thousands of people who received this treatment suffered serious brain damage. Many did not survive this assault on their brain and their humanity.

Insulin Coma Therapy

First introduced in the 1930s and used into the early 1970s, insulin coma therapy quickly gained widespread acceptance as an effective treatment for various forms of emotional distress, including schizophrenia. Insulin is a hormone we need to regulate our blood sugar levels. People with diabetes are unable to produce enough insulin in their bodies. Most diabetics need daily insulin injections to regulate their blood sugar. Excessive doses of insulin may reduce blood sugar to such a degree that a coma is induced. The rationale behind insulin coma therapy was to create a coma by dramatically reducing the person's blood sugar level. The coma was expected to somehow cure the person's emotional distress.

It was believed that the best results were obtained by using extremely high doses of insulin which put schizophrenic patients into life-threatening thirty- to fifty-hour comas. Dramatic results were claimed. It was not until twenty years later, by which time it was widely used, that a thorough study showed that insulin therapy had no therapeutic effect at all. It is now widely recognised within medicine that hypoglycemia (the medical term for low blood sugar) is a medical emergency. Every cell in the body, including brain cells, needs a constant supply of sugar to function normally and to survive. If a patient is deprived of glucose for more than two or three minutes, there is a real risk of permanent brain damage. Millions of people around the world treated with insulin coma therapy suffered serious brain damage as a consequence.

It took doctors more than twenty years to discover that insulin therapy was neither effective nor safe. Eventually this treatment was abandoned, but not without strong resistance from many psychiatrists.

Electro-Convulsive Treatment (ECT or 'Shock' Treatment)
ECT first gained popularity within modern medicine due

to the daft notion that epilepsy and depression were somehow illnesses which were diametrically opposite to each other. The medical logic was that depression could be cured by its polar opposite – seizures. This theory has never been proven and has largely been abandoned, though ECT is still a relatively common practice.

There is evidence that ECT causes considerable memory loss and permanent brain damage. In her book, *Out of Me: The Story of a Post-Natal Breakdown,* Fiona Shaw outlines her experience of severe post-natal depression. In graphic detail, she describes her hospital admissions and major loss of memory due to ECT treatments:

> The loss inflicted on me by ECT went far beyond ordinary forgetting. I lost the language of recollection, the capacity to give narrative shape or continuity to my life. I felt robbed of my autonomy, reliant on other people for material with which to shape any account. So Hugh [her husband] might come to visit me in the evening and I would ask him whom I'd seen that day and what I'd done. But once he'd told me, I was none the wiser. Sometimes I'd feel the faintest echo of recognition but that would be all. There was nothing there with which I could shape my thoughts. If only ECT brought its subjects out in a virulent rash, or made their hair fall out. Maybe then doctors would take its effects more seriously. As it is, most people receive the same kind of brush-off as I did. Queries are not regarded as legitimate doubts about the nature

and side effects of the treatment, but dismissed as the anxious product of the person's depression. All the more reason to get the electrodes on. When I questioned anybody about the possible longer-term effects of ECT on my memory, I was told it would have none. Yet it left a horrible brand on my mind and memory for another year and a half, maybe more.

Dr William Sargant was a prominent British psychiatrist at the time when ECT was first introduced. His enthusiasm for ECT contrasts sharply with Fiona Shaw's experience of this treatment. In his autobiography, *The Unquiet Mind,* published in 1967, Dr Sargant wrote:

Nowadays we may only need to prescribe four or five electric shock treatments, or some new antidepressant drug, whereupon the patient is himself again, without any need for elaborate case history or social investigation, still less the former eternity of talk.

A client of mine recently told me of her experiences of memory loss with ECT. Twenty years ago, she sought help from a psychiatrist for her depression. She had important university exams coming up a month later. The psychiatrist admitted her to hospital, treated her with eight ECT treatments, and then discharged her. Prior to her admission, she was depressed, but her memory was intact. On discharge, her memory was so impaired that her familiarity with her exam subjects was destroyed. Unable to recall the subject material, she decided not to sit the exams. Is there not a distinct possibility that a treatment which can cause such profound memory loss might also be damaging to the brain? There is research evidence that ECT causes brain damage in animals.

While less popular than it was a few decades ago, ECT is still used, particularly for what psychiatrists call severe or resistant depression. One might expect that a treatment as potentially damaging as ECT would be used only in a scientific way using clear and specific guidelines. Unfortunately, this is not always the case.

An audit of electro-convulsive treatment in two British National Health Service regions was published in the *British Journal of Psychiatry* in 1992. This audit, carried out by John Pippard, Mental Health Act Commissioner and Auditor Consultant at the Research Unit of the Royal College of Psychiatrists, uncovered some disturbing findings. He found that patients were twelve times more likely to receive ECT in some parts of England than in others. Patients in some hospitals received four times the seizure-inducing electrical impulse of those in other hospitals, the dose given being decided usually 'by habit, rather than rational strategy'. Few consultants were closely involved in the administration of ECT. John Pippard found that little had changed during the previous ten years in the unsatisfactory training and supervision of those who give the treatment.

Since the incidence of conditions for which ECT is used is fairly consistent from one region to the other, such a huge variance in the use of ECT has far more to do with the personal beliefs and preferences of the doctors involved than on any scientific basis. These disappointing results prompted the study's author to begin his research paper with the quotation: 'In medicine, what may start out as ignorance becomes practice if uncorrected.'

Prescribing Addictive and Dangerous Drugs

Amphetamines: This group of drugs first became available in the 1950s. They are now known to be highly dangerous and addictive. They fetch a high price on the black market. Since they were first introduced as medical treatments for emotional distress, millions of people around the world have become addicted to them. Many have died from their side effects. Yet they were easily available as slimming tablets with a doctor's prescription until the mid-1990s. The medical profession was slow to recognise the immense potential of these drugs to do harm.

Barbiturates, morphine, cocaine, opium and alcohol: In their day, each of these drugs was widely used for several decades by the medical profession. They were commonly prescribed as effective, safe and non-addictive treatments for a variety of conditions, particularly emotional distress, anxiety, and depression. With each drug, doctors were slow to realise how addictive they were. Rather than exercise caution regarding the possibility of addictiveness with each new drug, doctors presumed that each new drug was not addictive. These drugs were enthusiastically prescribed for several decades, leaving millions of drug addicts in their wake.

Tranquillizers and sleeping tablets: For over twenty years after they were introduced in the 1950s, tranquillizers (such as Valium, diazepam, Ativan and Xanax) and sleeping tablets (such as Dalmane, Mogadon, Rohypnol and Halcion) were widely prescribed by the medical profession. To this day, tranquillizers are one of the most prescribed groups of drugs worldwide. Doctors largely ignored the lessons which should have been learned from the legacy of addiction created by the over-prescription of morphine, barbiturates and amphetamines. As a result, the medical profession has created millions of drug addicts around the world: people who have become addicted to the treatments prescribed by their doctors, who assured them that these drugs were not addictive.

Even after the addictive potential of these tranquillizers became well recognised in the late 1980s, one such tranquillizer – Xanax – was heavily promoted by doctors in the early 1990s for the treatment of panic attacks. The medical experts advised that this drug was safe and free of any risk of addiction. They recommended treatment for several months at a time, even though the accepted guidelines for that group of drugs was for no more than four weeks of continuous treatment. The dosage recommended by the 'experts' was three to four times the previously recommended dosage range.

These experts got it very wrong. Promoting Xanax in this way was a huge marketing success, greatly increasing the use of the tranquillizer. But many people subsequently become addicted to the drug. It has been estimated that by the early 1990s, one and a half million new Xanax addicts were created every year in America alone via the doctor's prescription pad. Many of the people who now attend me are addicted to Xanax which was prescribed in high doses, with great enthusiasm, by either a psychiatrist or a GP. To this day I come across people whose doctors have prescribed Xanax for panic attacks, people who have been told by doctors that this drug is specifically designed for panic attacks. This statement is patently untrue. In *Toxic Psychiatry* Peter Breggin states that when a person stops taking tranquillizers, symptoms similar to but more severe than those for which the drug was first prescribed may be experienced. Moreover, Dr Breggin maintains that Upjohn, the company that manufacture Xanax, concealed important information about this tranquillizer:

On reading Upjohn's eight-page advertisements in psychiatric journals about its FDA studies, I was struck by something odd. At the top left of one page is the statement that drug evaluations were made at 'weeks 1,2,3,4,6 and 8 of therapy'. This gave the immediate impression that Xanax must have been proven effective at eight weeks. But the chart beneath this statement records only the first four weeks. Nowhere in the advertisement is there any discussion of the results after the full eight weeks. Then, at the bottom of the page, there is this explanation: 'Because of the high rate of placebo dropouts, week 4 was considered the study 'end point' for efficacy analyses.' In other words, Upjohn was counting only the first four weeks of the study and discarding the final results at eight weeks.

Why would Upjohn want to do that?

I was shocked at what I found in the original research report. By the end of the eight weeks, the sugar-pill patients were doing about as well as the drug patients. Indeed, the placebo patients were far better off, because they did not suffer the severe withdrawal and rebound reactions, including an increase in anxiety and in phobic responses, plus *a 350 percent greater number of panic attacks. In summary, the FDA Xanax study really shows that most patients were better off if they had never taken the drug.* [author's emphasis]

According to Dr Breggin, this dubious research was passed as acceptable by the American Food and Drug Administration (the FDA). Given how quickly Dr Breggin was able to identify serious flaws in this research, how did the FDA accept this research?

For five to ten years, many doctors embraced with great enthusiasm the idea of prescribing high doses of Xanax for people with high anxiety or panic. Towards the end of the 1990s, this trend declined. Few doctors would prescribe Xanax in such high doses now. But the warning signs of tranquillizer addiction and ineffectiveness were there before this disastrous overprescribing of Xanax for anxiety and panic began. I clearly recall my own reaction ten years ago to the vigorous pushing of this new 'break-through' by the drug company's representatives when they visited me, as they did with all practising GPs. I was not convinced. I was suspicious: how could it be right to prescribe very high doses of tranquillizers for several months and presume they were not addictive? I did not buy into the idea at all. I remember, months later, trying the high-dose Xanax regime reluctantly with one person, whose panic *did* reduce somewhat. But her anxiety reduced because she was so sedated by the tranquillizers. I decided there and then that I would never use high-dose Xanax again.

Many of my medical colleagues – psychiatrists and GPs alike – did accept that high-dose Xanax was a breakthrough in the treatment of anxiety and prescribed it for many years and with great enthusiasm. The medical profession should have known better. Yet the whole debacle has died a quiet death. The medical profession has not been called to account for this grievous error of judgement.

In *Confessions of a Medical Heretic* (1979) American doctor Robert Mendlesohn describes a peculiarity regarding the side effects of Valium and other drugs. His comments apply to all commonly prescribed tranquillizers:

> You should be aware of all the drugs for which the side effects are the same as the indications. For example, if you read the list of indications for Valium, and then read the list of side effects, you'll find that the lists are more or less interchangeable! Under the indications you'll find: anxiety, fatigue, depression, acute agitation, tremors, hallucinosis, skeletal muscle spasms. And under the side effects: anxiety, fatigue, depression, acute agitation, tremors,

hallucinations, increased muscle spasticity! I
admit I don't know how to use a drug like this:
what am I supposed to do if I prescribe it and
the symptoms continue? Stop the drug or
double the dose? What strategy lies behind
using drugs like this is a mystery to me.

Doctors speak with confidence about the currently accepted treatments – antidepressants like Prozac, Seroxat,
Favarin and others. In ten or twenty years, will the
treatments which today's experts speak of so highly have
been found out? Will they be found to be useless, harmful
or addictive like most of the 'treatments' of the past?
According to Charles Medawar, the addictive potential of
these newer antidepressant drugs – the SSRIs (Selective
Serotonin Reuptake Inhibitors) – is a cause for concern.
In his previously mentioned article in the February 1998
edition of *What Doctors Don't Tell You*, Medawar wrote:

The number of Yellow Card reports do suggest
a problem. After 17 years of use, the benzo-
diazepines (tranquillizers) had attracted 28
Yellow Card reports of suspected withdrawal
problems, while the numbers of reports relating
to SSRIs in less than ten years (as of March
1997) were pushing the 1,000 mark and rising.

The main method used to assess untoward problems with
new drugs is the 'Yellow Card' system. Doctors are asked
to complete a yellow form if they suspect that a drug has
caused side effects. This system is casually implemented:

even in the widely publicised thalidomide disaster of the 1960s, when thousands of newborn babies suffered major limb deformities due to the drug thalidomide, fewer than twenty Yellow Cards about this drug were returned by doctors. The public – for whom new drugs are prescribed and recommended by doctors – are the guinea-pigs. Doctors will not usually downplay a medication unless another medication becomes available as a replacement. When the SSRIs became available toward the end of the 1980s, the medical profession and the pharmaceutical industry had a new great white hope to turn to. Since then, the SSRIs have become the core of treatment for virtually all the conditions which just fifteen years ago were being treated with tranquillizers: anxiety, panic, agoraphobia and other phobias, obsessive-compulsive disorders and eating disorders. Until the end of the 1980s, tranquillizers were also recommended and widely prescribed for depression.

Since virtually all other long-term medications previously prescribed for these conditions (with the possible exception of the older antidepressants) have been largely discredited, the SSRIs and other newer antidepressant drugs are the only medication the medical profession has to offer. Since no revolutionary or miracle drug is currently waiting in the wings to replace the SSRIs, the medical profession will vehemently stick to their guns about the effectiveness, safety and non-addictiveness of these drugs. Whatever about the public needing to take Prozac and its equivalents, the medical profession certainly needs the public to believe in these drugs, because right now, the medical profession has little else to offer.

Medical experts repeatedly tell the public that the psychiatric system works. The public have no way of checking this out for themselves. If a GP or psychiatrist is being interviewed on the radio, and several people phone in to express how the medical treatment of their 'mental illness' did not work for them (and I have heard several such radio shows), the doctor can reply with a statistic which cannot be debated because only medical professionals have this information. For example, on media programmes about depression, I have heard doctors state that the medical profession knows for sure that antidepressants are 70 per cent effective. The implication is that those who did not respond were therefore part of the other 30 per cent. I used to believe that too, but not any more. My personal experience of twenty years working as a medical doctor suggests to me that the effectiveness of antidepressants is significantly less than 70 per cent.

Long-stay psychiatric in-patients are a particularly vulnerable group. Written off by society as 'mad', they have no voice. Long forgotten by the outside world, they have become dependent on their carers. The 1998 report of the Inspectorate of Mental Hospitals in Ireland revealed some worrying findings. The report found that the number of mental health patients – particularly long-term patients – who were on numerous drugs simultaneously and often at high doses was striking. Moreover, the Inspectorate observed that the number of sudden deaths in psychiatric hospitals appeared to be increasing. The Inspectorate commented that some of these deaths were attributed to drug-related side effects. They found that drug-prescribing was often arbitrary and made without regard to appropriate clinical diagnosis and that in some cases no notes had been entered in patients' charts during the previous four years. For good reasons, I am sure, the Inspectorate expressed its intention that a greater number of inspections of mental health services should be un-announced, as opposed to the usual practice of giving two to three days' notice. The Inspectorate also mentioned that three out of four acute psychiatric admissions were for people who had previous psychiatric hospital ad-missions. This figure confirms the 'revolving door' of psychiatry, and raises questions about the effectiveness of psychiatric treatment. If in-patient psychiatric treat-ment was truly effective, why would so many patients need readmission?

Psychiatry has overcome psychology in the battle for the expert's chair. Psychiatry now sees itself as a modern scientific medical specialty, standing proud and tall alongside cardiology, gastroenterology, neurology and the other medical specialties. This position has given psych-iatry a respectability and status which puts it almost above questioning. The counselling professions have not yet managed to create such status and position. Psych-iatry has therefore firmly established itself as the field of expertise in 'mental illness'. The benefits to the victor – psychiatry – are enormous. The winner takes all. Psych-iatry now effectively owns and dominates all aspects of treating emotional distress, 'mental illness' and suicide.

When suicide is discussed in the media, the expert involved in the programme or article is usually a psych-iatrist. For instance, RTÉ's *Late Late Show* devoted an entire programme to suicide in 1997. During the two-and-a-half-hour discussion, two psychiatrists sat alongside presenter Gay Byrne. Throughout the programme, these doctors were portrayed as the acknowledged experts on suicide. Both psychiatrists spoke at length, and the presenter regularly asked them for their opinions.

There was no room for a psychologist on this panel of experts, not even for the president of the Psychological Society of Ireland, Pauline Beegin. She had to be content with sitting in the audience. While the psychiatrists were given freedom to speak frequently and at length during the programme, the president of the Psychological Society of Ireland had only one brief opportunity to speak. In my opinion, hers was one of the most important contributions to the entire two-and-a-half-hour programme.

Concerned about psychiatry's domination of suicide, Pauline Beegin said:

> Listening to the two psychiatrists, one of the issues I have difficulty with is the whole description of suicide as an illness, or looking at the problems that cause suicide as illnesses, because I believe they are emotional problems that need to be dealt with. One of the things about rural areas [she was responding to the interviewer's question, which was about suicide in rural areas] is access to talking to anybody about emotional events that have gotten out of control in your life, that you can't get perspective on, the fear of being labelled as schizophrenic or psychiatrically ill puts people off, they can't deal with the stigma, and they

don't know who to turn to. The psychologist or psychiatrist is in the local psychiatric hospital which for most people in rural communities is not accessible because they are identified so easily. People are scared that word will get out that they are attending the psychiatrist, that they have a so-called 'psychiatric illness'.

These cautionary words from an experienced psychologist received no further attention during this two-and-a-half-hour programme. Gay Byrne quickly moved on to speak to another member of the audience. At no time during the remainder of the programme did Gay Byrne or the two expert psychiatrists refer back to Pauline Beegin's comments. Views which oppose those of psychiatry are easily rebuffed, or as happened on this important television programme, ignored.

What Pauline Beegin was really objecting to was the medicalisation of suicide. To medicalise a problem means to categorise it as a medical issue. Medical doctors then become the experts to whom the public turn for advice and direction. For example, the prevailing medical view – as expressed by Professor Patricia Casey on the afore-mentioned *Late Late Show* on suicide – describes alcohol abuse and drug addiction as 'psychiatric disorders':

About 80 to 90 per cent of suicides have a diagnosable psychiatric disorder; depressive illness particularly, alcohol abuse, increasingly drug abuse, and schizophrenia. These are the principal conditions.

My view is that alcohol and drug abuse are largely emotional and psychological problems rather than 'psychiatric disorders'.

Psychiatry significantly influences government and health department's initiatives on mental illness. Since 1992 there has been a 'Beat Depression' health campaign in full swing in Britain and to a lesser extent in Ireland. These campaigns have been driven by psychiatry. The main treatment recommended in these campaigns has been drug treatment. Psychiatry and its prevailing views dominated the two major reports into suicide carried out in Ireland in recent years: the *Report of the National Task Force on Suicide* (1998), and *Suicide in Ireland; A Global Perspective and a National Strategy* (1998). The views of psychology receive little attention in these highly publicised projects.

With the financial backing of the pharmaceutical industry, psychiatry's consensus view dominates research into 'mental illness' and suicide. Consequently, psychiatry effectively directs the treatment of 'mental illness' in the future, having already secured control of 'mental illness' in the present. And by bringing suicide into the category of 'mental illness', modern medicine has seized hold of suicide and suicide research. Psychiatry is unassailable at the top of the tree, and the patient is at the bottom of the pecking order.

In the foreword to Jeffrey Masson's *Against Therapy* (1997) the aforementioned psychologist Dorothy Rowe describes the hierarchical order which greeted her when she began working in Britain, early in her career:

When I first came to England in 1968 from Australia, I went to work at a university psychiatric clinic where the professor and the other consultant psychiatrists were devotees of the medical model of mental illness. There, the psychologist's role was to administer psychological tests, the psychiatrist's role was to diagnose mental illness, prescribe drugs, and to supervise the administration of electroconvulsive therapy (shock treatment) and the occasional lobotomy. All this came as a surprise to me. It was strange to find myself among men who maintained their prestige in a strict hierarchy in which, on the lowest rung, the patients had no hope of advancement, and who believed that despair and fear are caused not by the terrors of this world but by an aberrant metabolism or gene.

Little has changed in the hierarchy of psychiatry since Dorothy Rowe experienced this in 1968. Nowadays there are both male and female psychiatrists, but the dominant position of the psychiatrist remains. Psychiatrists make the decisions. They are the experts and are beyond questioning. I have seen this over and over again during my medical career. According to the medical model, the doctor knows best. The patient – especially the psychiatric patient – does not know best. Patients must rely on the doctor to find out what is wrong with them and prescribe the right treatment.

In a case which unfortunately typifies the experience of many patients, a woman was admitted to a leading Irish psychiatric unit, having been diagnosed with severe clinical depression. She was admitted under the care of an eminent psychiatrist. During her three-week admission, her contact with her psychiatrist consisted of two brief (less than five minutes) visits per week. These consultations consisted of a short 'Hello, how are you' and a review of the patient's medication. During these brief meetings, the consultant was accompanied by an entourage of doctors and nurses, which hardly encouraged the patient to speak frankly to the psychiatrist.

The medication did not help. The patient and her family were very disappointed that this was all the psychiatrist had to offer. Eight weeks after she was discharged, she remained as depressed as ever, despite taking the antidepressants as prescribed. Then her husband became ill with asthma. Her depression improved dramatically. Suddenly, she felt needed. Her depression was not and had never been a biological, physical illness. It was an emotional withdrawal reaction. Having no sense of self-worth, one of the few ways she could feel any sense of importance in life was by caring for others. Her children were grown up and had flown the nest. She was in her fifties. She had no one to look after any more. She became depressed because she felt worthless, not because of any brain abnormality. When her husband became ill, she had someone to look after again and her depression quickly lifted.

Hospital policies regarding how the 'mentally ill' are cared for are largely in the hands of psychiatrists. So is the care of the 'mentally ill' in the community. The diagnoses and treatments which psychiatrists arrive at each day have to be accepted without question by the other concerned parties – the GP, the psychologist, the social worker, the psychiatric nurse. In the management of a patient, if the psychologist disagrees with the views of the psychiatrist, one of two things usually happens:

- The psychologist keeps his opinion to himself, just as many schoolchildren hesitate to stand up to their all-powerful teacher.
- The psychologist expresses his opinion. Whether or not this opinion is well received by the psychiatrist, typically the psychiatrist's opinion wins out.

Psychiatrists frequently state that psychiatric treatment is now a team effort – psychologists, occupational therapists, GPs and other health-care workers operating together in the treatment of 'mental illness'. But the policies and philosophies of this team are dominated by one member of the team: the psychiatrist. When psychiatrists and psychologists do work together, the hierarchical order is clear to both. The psychiatrist is in charge. Psychiatric beliefs rule. The psychologist plays a small part in the action. Being at the top of the tree of mental-care treatment gives psychiatry great power. Psychiatry has become very powerful and regularly wields its power, often in ways so subtle it goes unnoticed.

Medical training is a significant part of the problem. Most medical students come from privileged and stable backgrounds, and few would have much personal experience of the severe emotional distress they will later encounter in their patients. In order to study hard enough to achieve the high exam results necessary to enter medical school, many students have led a somewhat closeted teenage existence, a pattern which is continued during the very demanding years at medical school.

From the moment these teenagers enter medical school, they are indoctrinated into a medical system which places great emphasis on the physical, biological aspects of human existence. For six years, these students learn an enormous amount of information about physical aspects of medicine such as anatomy, physiology, pathology and drug treatments. Even when students learn about psychiatry, what they learn is not an exploration of the emotional, psychological and social aspects of human existence, nor indeed the daily struggles of relationships and everyday life. Rather, the focus is on psychiatry as a scientific branch of medicine, where people's problems are evaluated in the language of psychiatric illness. The young students emerge as qualified doctors, already highly conditioned into the medical, biological approach. Their postgraduate training further cements their preoccupation with the biological aspects of the human being. They believe that they are scientists, but many have already lost a key scientific attribute – open-mindedness. They think they are open-minded, but they look at patients through the tinted glasses of their medical training. The combination of authoritarian teaching and peer competition breeds conforming medical students and doctors. Free thinking and questioning are not encouraged in medical schools. Increasingly, there is a trend away from psychotherapy towards drug treatments. Particularly in America, many prestigious medical schools which used to include psychotherapy as part of psychiatric training no longer do so. Consequently, increasing numbers of psychiatrists are emerging from their training with little understanding of or respect for psychotherapy.

Perhaps it is not surprising that more than fifty clinical trials of new drugs were conducted on psychiatric patients in Ireland over the past three years. Was anything like that number of trials into the effectiveness of psychotherapy carried out in Irish hospitals over the same period? Somehow, I doubt it.

'IF ONLY WE COULD GIVE PATIENTS MORE TIME'

Building up trusting relationships with people requires that doctors or therapists must be prepared to set aside sufficient time for their clients. GPs' waiting rooms are typically full of people – how could a GP possibly give patients more than a quarter of an hour of his time? I believe it comes down to priorities. I might have forty things I would like to do tomorrow, but I will be doing well if I get to twenty of these. I will give attention to what I see as most important. The rest have to wait for another day.

We all manage to give time to what is most important to us. Doctors say they do not have enough time to give their patients. If doctors have not created a working environment designed to give their patients enough time, it is because giving patients more time is not high enough on the medical profession's priority list. Giving people enough time in the consultation was so important to me that I dramatically changed how I work. I have made giving an hour to people my first priority. If I can do it, so can other doctors – if it is important enough to them. Where there is a will, there is usually a way.

Giving clients time is a core value of the counselling and psychotherapy professions – hence the standard hour-long consultation. GPs do not prioritise the duration of the consultation as much, therefore their patients get ten to fifteen minutes. Behind plaintive cries of 'if only I had more time to give my patients' lies a reluctance to take the steps necessary to provide people with longer consult-ations.

In my opinion, the principal reason why doctors give people so little time relates to their income. Extending the duration of consultations inevitably means seeing fewer patients per day. Doctors would have to reduce their patient list size, reducing their income in the process. A 1993 study funded by the American Psychiatric Associ-ation reported that psychiatrists who practice psycho-therapy cannot make much more than $100,000 per annum, whereas a practice confined to medication and evaluation will yield $300,000 over the same period.

In the following two chapters, I present an alternative view. This view questions the very existence of 'psych-iatric illness'. I explore whether so-called 'psychiatric illness' might instead be an understandable reaction to difficult or intolerable life circumstances. I ask whether life itself, our experiences and our relationships, may trigger the deep emotional distress which is labelled as 'mental illness' by the medical profession.

I believe that the degree to which children's physical, emotional, psychological and social needs are not met has a bearing on their risk of developing so-called 'mental illness' later in life. This is not to suggest that parents are to blame. I believe that most parents do their level best for their children. But parenting is a tough task. With the best will in the world, important childhood needs can go unnoticed and unmet.

Children frequently repress their emotional pain because it can be overwhelming. They grow into adults who try to protect themselves from further hurt and emotional pain. But the early years of frightening solitude make them vulnerable to a major emotional distress reaction if they continue to feel hurt as their adult life unfolds. Relationships with parents do not always improve, often becoming more painful as the years go by. The daughter who since early childhood has been terrified of her aggressive father still yearns for the father's unexpressed love in her forties. But her father is now in his sixties, and old habits die hard. Every time she sees her father, she experiences a maelstrom of emotions: fear, anger, regret, love, loss and above all, loneliness. It still hurts to be reminded every time she sees him that they will never be close.

A study presented to the 1999 winter meeting of the Irish division of the Royal College of Psychiatrists highlighted how childhood emotional trauma can lead to 'psychiatric illness' later in life. The psychiatrist Professor Anthony Clare and colleagues found that 37 per cent of depressed women attending their GP were sexually abused as children. The likelihood of adult depression paralleled the degree of sexual abuse. More serious sexual abuse – involving penetration – led to depression in 100 per cent of cases.

I recall a twenty-year-old girl who attended me once. She had suffered from depression for years, had had ECT more than ten times, and a series of antidepressants without improvement. She quickly informed me that she had been to several psychiatrists, and everyone (including herself) was satisfied that there was no identifiable cause for her depression. While she spoke with an air of confidence and assuredness, beneath her words was a sense of fear, and she had showed a pattern of withdrawal over many years. I sensed that she was much more vulnerable than she was prepared to admit to me, and perhaps to herself. While exploring her childhood, she assured me that she came from a happy home. It emerged that she had absolutely no recollection of her childhood up to the age of nine. For any person, this would seem odd, but for a twenty-year-old it was particularly strange to have no recollection of half of her life. I wondered whether something might have happened to her in her early childhood that was so awful, she had to black out her whole memory of childhood. Could there have been child abuse in her past? There were many people coming and going in her home – many people had access to her besides her parents. I didn't go into this with her, though I suggested that if she was willing, we might explore her childhood further during later consultations. She did not make another appointment. Perhaps she did not like or trust me enough to speak to me about this. Perhaps she thought I didn't have a clue, though she did seem to warm to me during the consultation. Or perhaps she didn't want her view of her endogenous depression threatened. Maybe she really needed to protect herself from the pain she may have blanked out for years. No doctor had been previously struck by this total lack of childhood memories.

Later in life, there are many triggers which may bring the repressed emotional pain closer to the surface: relationships whose passion has faded into monotony as lovers drift apart; mothers at home feeling they are taken for granted; men and women who derive little satisfaction from their work but feel they must stay in the job to pay the bills or maintain their social status; women who would love to have children but cannot, who experience great pain every time their friends talk about their children; bereavements or other life events that generate seismic changes, great insecurity or emotional pain in people's lives. For many people, the world we live in can be a cruel place. The process by which emotional distress is translated into 'mental illness' is discussed in the following two chapters.

3
—

DEPRESSION

According to the World Health Organisation, depression will become the world's most pervasive serious illness by the year 2020. Currently, depression effects 340 million people worldwide, accounting for one-third of psychiatric hospital admissions. Given the scale of the problem of depression, it behoves the medical profession to investigate depression thoroughly and holistically. However, the medical profession has become so preoccupied with establishing that depression is caused by a biochemical brain imbalance that the possibility that life experiences may cause depression has been largely neglected. Attracted by the alluring theory that depression may be genetic, the prevailing medical view disregards an obvious possibility. Children growing up in a home where one or both parents have depression may themselves be prone to depression because of the knock-on effects of their family situation on their childhood and later life. It is widely known that if a mother is terrified of lightning and frantically gathers her children under the stairs in a thunderstorm, her children may also dread lightning. I have never heard anyone suggest that their increased likelihood of dreading lightning is due to an inherited genetic defect. Similarly, people's political affiliation, career choice and religious beliefs are frequently influenced by the family environment. Yet there is rarely any suggestion that these influences are genetic. It is well known that children who have been physically abused in childhood are at risk of repeating that pattern of abuse with their own children. Again, this repeating of patterns is thought to be due to their previous experiences rather than genetic inheritance. Why, then, do we presume that the increased incidence of depression in children of depressed parents is genetically inherited? People who become depressed are not 'mentally ill'. They are trying to cope with living as best they can, having experienced more than their fair share of hurt, loneliness and rejection.

DIAGNOSING DEPRESSION

Psychiatrists the world over look to *The Diagnostic and Statistical Manual* (*DSM*) – put together by panels of psychiatrists convened by the American Psychiatric Association – as the guide to diagnosing psychiatric illness. According to the fourth and most up-to-date edition (2000), a 'major depressive episode' is diagnosed in the presence of the following criteria. Judge for yourself whether these criteria are scientific, or whether they are merely descriptions of understandable human feelings and behaviours, in the following extract from the *DSM*:

Criterion A1: The mood in a major depressive episode is often described by the depressive person as depressed, sad, hopeless, discouraged, or 'down in the dumps'. In some cases, sadness may be denied at first, but may subsequently be elicited by interview (e.g. by pointing out that the individual looks as if he or she is about to cry). In some individuals who complain of feeling 'blah', having no feelings or feeling anxious, the presence of a depressed mood can be inferred from the person's facial expression and demeanour. Some individuals emphasise somatic complaints (bodily aches and pains, for example) rather than reporting feelings of sadness. Many individuals report or exhibit increased irritability.

Criterion A2: Loss of interest or pleasure is nearly always present, at least to some degree. Individuals may report feeling less interested in hobbies (e.g. a former avid golfer no longer plays, a child who used to enjoy soccer finds excuses not to practice).

Criterion A3: Appetite is usually reduced... (but) other individuals... may have increased appetite... there may be significant loss or gain in weight.

Criterion A4: The most common sleep disturbance associated with a major depressive episode is insomnia. Less frequently, individuals present with oversleeping (hypersomnia). Sometimes, the reason that the individual seeks treatment is for the disturbed sleep.

Criterion A5: Psychomotor changes including

agitation (e.g. the inability to sit still)... or retardation (e.g. slowed speech, thinking or body movements).

Criterion A6: Decreased energy, tiredness and fatigue are common.

Criterion A7: The sense of worthlessness or guilt associated with a major depressive episode may include unrealistic negative evaluations of one's worth or guilty preoccupations or ruminations over minor past failings.

Criterion A8: Many individuals report impaired ability to think, concentrate or make decisions... They appear easily distracted or complain of memory difficulties.

Criterion A9: Frequently, there may be thoughts of death, suicide ideation, or suicide attempts.

According to this *Diagnostic and Statistical Manual*, a formal diagnosis of a major depressive episode can be made when two conditions are considered:

- The severity and duration of the depressive state (criterion A1)
- Four of the remaining eight criteria being present

Who decided that to diagnose depression, criterion A1 plus four more criteria needed to be met? Why did they select five criteria as the magic figure? What is so different between a person who meets six criteria – and is therefore diagnosed as having a major depressive episode and needing antidepressant treatment – and one who meets four criteria, and therefore receives no psychiatric diagnosis or treatment? Why five criteria? Why not three? Or seven? How valid are these criteria?

There is nothing scientific about diagnosing depression. There is no valid scientific means of explaining why five criteria result in a diagnosis of a major depressive episode, while three or four criteria being met is normal, requiring no diagnosis or treatment. Many of the criteria for diagnosing a major depressive episode – believed by doctors to be a severe psychiatric illness – are understandable human reactions to situations and events encountered in life. Individuals complaining of feeling 'blah', children who do not want to play football any more, people looking as though they are about to cry, feeling sad, hopeless, down in the dumps – does this sound scientific?

These are the official guidelines of the American Psychiatric Association, the best these experts can formulate. Even if doctors stuck faithfully to these guidelines, there is huge scope for misdiagnosis, such is the vagueness of these criteria. But many doctors who prescribe antidepressant drugs every day of the week do not refer to these guidelines when diagnosing depression.

The Diagnostic and Statistical Manual is looked upon within modern medicine with the same reverence as the Bible is by Christian religions. Yet, as British psychologist and author Lucy Johnstone points out in her book *Users and Abusers of Psychiatry*, the *DSM* leaves a lot to be desired.

> Psychiatrists strive very hard to present psychiatry
> as a legitimate and respectable branch of medical

science, so that they can maintain their claim that the psychiatric service must be headed by doctors rather than, say, nurses or social workers or a team of professionals working as equals. This means that there is an overriding emphasis on diagnosing, labelling, and categorising patients and prescribing medical-type solutions, rather than exploring feelings and relationships. The prime example of this is the *Diagnostic and Statistical Manual of Mental Disorders,* Third Edition (known as *DSM-III*), the psychiatrist's guide to diagnosis, which in 472 pages labels and divides psychiatric problems into literally hundreds of sections and sub-sections in a manner which in a patient would be seen as a sign of obsessive-compulsive disorder. The same attitude is evident in many psychiatric textbooks.

Before his untimely death, in his final *Sunday Independent* article on 5 March 2000, Jonathan Philbin Bowman described *The Diagnostic and Statistical Manual* as 'the book that helps doctors stop thinking, and it certainly helps them stop feeling'.

The confusion within medicine regarding the diagnosis of depression is well illustrated by Charles Medawar. He has researched depression and doctors' antidepressant-prescribing habits in great detail. In his *Antidepressant Web* internet site he concluded:

Perhaps the most unifying definition of 'depression' is that it is a condition to be treated

with antidepressant drugs. There may not be a
lot to distinguish between the drugs, but there
is no end of possibilities for prescribing them.

It appears that I am not the only person with major
reservations about how doctors diagnose so-called 'psychiatric illnesses'. And while doctors rarely speak of the role
of stress as a cause of depression, psychiatrists themselves do not seem united regarding the link between
stressful life events and depression. In the *Irish Independent*
of 6 May 2000, Professor Patricia Casey is quoted as saying
that 'at least 50 per cent of people that I treat [for depres-
sion] have absolutely no triggers or traumas. In these cases,
depression occurs out of the blue.' Yet Limerick psychiatrist Dr Pat Doyle wrote in the *Irish Medical News* of 6
December 1999 that 'research has shown that in an
individual with multiple episodes of depression, the first
one or two episodes are generally stress-determined.' The
profession has chosen to focus almost entirely on drug
treatments to the expense of stress research and stress-
treatment strategies. When people attend their doctors
and depression is diagnosed, drug treatment is almost
always the first treatment offered.

'DO YOU WANT SOMETHING FOR IT?'

The diagnosis of depression is often based on a casual
exchange between doctor and patient, as Rachel experienced when she visited her GP:

GP:　　　　'Rachel, do you think you might be depressed?'
Rachel:　　'Yes, I suppose I could be.'

GP: 'Would you like to take a course of anti-
             depressants for a while?'

Rachel: 'No, I'd prefer to get over this without medi-
             cation if at all possible.'

This type of casual negotiation is a common occurrence in the GP's surgery. The conversation has an innocent, friendly quality about it, but this is deceptive. Rachel refused the offer of antidepressant drugs so there was no more said about it. Had she accepted the medication, this casual chat would soon become a definite psychiatric diagnosis. Six months later, the fact that the GP offered the antidepressants as one might offer someone a cup of tea would be long forgotten. Had Rachel taken the anti-depressants, this would in the future be taken as evidence that Rachel suffered from depression, a 'mental illness'. After all, why would a patient take antidepressants if she did not have depression? Her chart would state that she has depression, which may affect her life in many ways.

This 'diagnosis' might reduce her chances of future employment or insurance cover. A prospective relation-ship partner might shy away if he found out that she has been diagnosed as having a 'mental illness'. If Rachel found herself in the GP's surgery three years later with complaints that even vaguely suggested that she was depressed, the GP would quickly recall that Rachel had previously needed antidepressants, and so conclude that this was obviously a recurrence of her known depressive illness. Had Rachel taken the antidepressants, she would have been labelled for life. By refusing the prescription, she did herself one big favour. Rachel's problems were caused by a very troubled relationship with her mother, who demanded that Rachel be always at her beck and call, and gave thirty-five-year-old Rachel little freedom to create an independent life for herself.

Diagnosis and treatment based on subtle negotiation also regularly takes place with patients who come to the doctor because of stress and anxiety. Pauline was going through a tough patch in her life. After years of marital disharmony, she finally decided that enough was enough. The time had come to leave her husband. For twelve months she was under intense stress, striving to create a life for herself and looking after her two children on her own. One day, while attending her GP with one of her children, the doctor asked her how she was coping. Pauline said that things were tough, but she was getting through it. Her GP asked Pauline if she wanted something to help her cope with the stress. That 'something' was a tranquillizer, which Pauline wisely refused. Pauline was coping; she did not need addictive tranquillizers. Pauline needed her wits about her then more than at any other time in her life. How would drugs which would sedate her help her through this challenging time? Yet doctors get away with this type of practice regularly. Many's the person who, when asked 'do you want something for your anxiety?' said 'yes' and ended up addicted to tranquillizers, worse off than before they took them – with an addiction created by the medical profession.

A friend related the following story to me. A middle-aged woman friend of hers became quite emotionally distressed due to difficult events in her life, events which were also affecting her husband's emotional well-being.

She attended her GP for help. The doctor quickly prescribed Prozac for her. On hearing that her husband was also upset, the doctor prescribed Prozac for him, without even talking to the man. Shocked at the doctor's casual attitude towards the prescription of Prozac, neither of them took the tablets. That GP lost two patients.

'CLINICAL' DEPRESSION

'Clinical' depression is a term which has gained popularity with both the medical profession and the public. This term has no specific definition. It is usually understood to mean that the person in question is sufficiently depressed to ensure that the diagnosis is definite and unquestionable. The term 'clinical' conjures up images of doctors and hospitals. The medical profession is known to approach health in a 'clinical' fashion. The phrase 'clinical depression' instantly labels the sufferer as having a medical problem, a definite 'mental illness'. People who question the medical profession's approach to depression are easily rebuffed. Now that depression is 'clinical', how dare anyone challenge the views of medical clinicians in their own field of expertise, clinical medicine! Yet, as I mentioned earlier, no tests are carried out to confirm this 'clinical' diagnosis, because no such tests exist.

Patients and their relatives are more likely to acquiesce to taking antidepressant drugs once they are told that their depression is 'clinical'. This term implies that the patient cannot understand what is going on since it is a clinical (i.e. medical) problem. The patient should really just keep taking the tablets and leave the rest to the experts. Power shifts from the patient to the doctor, decreasing the patient's understanding of what is going on. Their input into their own recovery is reduced. Rather than being a 'mental illness', 'clinical depression' is frequently misdiagnosed – as in the following case histories.

Two Cases of 'Clinical' Depression

Jim took early retirement from work at fifty-five years of age. Always used to being busy, he did not know how to occupy all his new-found free time. He soon became depressed and anxious, withdrawing into himself. He became irritable with his family. Jim's GP diagnosed that Jim was clinically depressed and antidepressants were prescribed. These drugs numbed Jim's feelings. Two months later, Jim felt less anxious but his depression remained. In an effort to overcome his depression, he then came to see me.

It quickly emerged that Jim tended to become depressed when confronted with major life changes. Insecure since his childhood, Jim needed a great deal of security and predictability in his life. Major life changes increased his sense of insecurity, resulting in Jim becoming depressed. I felt that there was nothing 'clinical' about Jim's depression. Jim's retirement closed the door on his working life. I felt he needed to create new meaning and purpose in this new phase of his life. We discussed various possibilities. Jim decided to become involved in several community activities. He made new friends and now has a busy, vibrant life. Off all medication and no longer depressed, Jim has a renewed sense of security and predictability in his life.

Twenty-year-old Paul was coming to the end of his

second year at university. Having sailed through the first year, Paul did not anticipate any hitches. All went well until the week before the exams, when Paul became very uptight. He could not sleep and was too nervous to eat. Paul sat the exams but was extremely anxious throughout. He performed far worse than he would have expected and ended up failing. Then his personality seemed to change. Paul became withdrawn, even from his closest friends. He stayed in bed until late afternoon, having no interest in anything. He blamed himself over and over again for being such a fool: for screwing up the exams, his life and his family.

In Dublin he was referred to a psychiatrist, who concluded that Paul was suffering from clinical depression, for which he needed antidepressant drugs. These drugs were the only treatment the psychiatrist recommended. In a letter to me, the psychiatrist wrote: 'Because of his clinical depression I have put him on an antidepressant.' A repeat appointment was arranged for three weeks later, at which the psychiatrist briefly asked Paul more about the tablets than about himself. The next appointment was scheduled for three months later.

As often happens, the psychiatrist misread the situation. Paul did not feel comfortable with the psychiatrist, who asked Paul a list of leading questions, questions which did not invite him to open up. Consequently, the 'expert' doctor did not even get a glimpse of how distressed Paul really was. Because of how he approached Paul, the psychiatrist did not grasp that Paul was suicidal. At the time when Paul was at his lowest ebb, the psychiatrist decided that Paul did not need to see him again for three months.

Paul decided to make the 120-mile journey to attend me at frequent intervals. I had been Paul's GP when he was younger. He felt he could trust me. The psychiatrist was on his doorstep, but Paul had no desire to return to see him again.

We built up a trusting relationship. I soon realised that Paul's exam crisis had nothing to do with 'clinical' depression. He had experienced a performance anxiety reaction, a severe anxiety reaction engendered by an intense fear of not performing well in his exams. Performance-related anxiety is quite common. It occurs in people who have had reason at some time in their lives to seriously doubt their ability to perform, to get it right. Paul's performance-related anxiety went right back to his early schooldays, when he had major difficulties for three years in dealing with one very authoritarian teacher. His confidence in his own ability to perform suffered hugely as a result. Throughout his childhood, Paul compensated by putting twice as much effort into his schoolwork rather than experience the humiliation he felt at the hands of that teacher.

By trying so hard, Paul got by in school. His parents understandably thought that his childhood experiences were over and done with, but the underlying emotional wounds never healed. Under the surface, he had remained terrified of failing. This fear rebounded on him in his second year in college. Paul did not need antidepressant drugs. He needed a great deal of support and compassion to help him come to his own understanding of the experience. Only then could he see that there was light at the end of the tunnel. Nine months later, the crisis was over. Paul passed the repeat examinations and returned to college. He received a great deal of support from his family and from me.

Paul did not take the antidepressants, but he recovered. Having overcome the shock of failing his exams, Paul re-established contact with many of the friends from whom he had withdrawn. He now knows that his unique worth as a human being cannot be erased by the results of one exam.

The psychiatrist incorrectly interpreted Paul's behaviour as signs of 'clinical' depression. This medical expert missed the point. Paul withdrew from people not because he was mentally ill, but because he felt humiliated and overwhelmed. Paul believed that he had lost face in the eyes of his friends so he could not bring himself to meet them. All his friends passed the exams. They were all cheerfully planning their summer holidays. The only thing Paul had to look forward to was repeating his exams. It is hardly surprising – and certainly not a sign of a 'mental illness' – that he needed to withdraw from his friends and from life.

Living involves a continuous interplay between mind and body. Our bodies continuously respond to our minute-by-minute emotional state. I have known several previously healthy people who died suddenly as a result of over-whelmingly sad news. It is true that depression can be accompanied by a slowing down of bodily activity and functions. But it does not automatically follow that depression is a clinical, physical illness. Equally plausibly, the bodily slowing-down could be the result of the person's emotional state.

Some years ago, I referred a fifteen-year-old girl who was going through an emotional crisis to a psychiatrist. At the first consultation, the psychiatrist diagnosed depression. He put the girl, Claire, on two medications: an antidepressant and tranquillizers. She attended the psychiatrist five times. Each follow-up consultation focused more on the drug treatment than on her. The psychiatrist commented in a letter to me that Claire was 'extremely self-critical and had self-esteem difficulties which mainly relate to weight problems. She is quite sensitive to teasing, and this seems to be happening to some extent in school at present.'

In these two sentences, the psychiatrist actually described the kernel of Claire's problem: extremely low self-esteem, severe self-criticism, a very negative self-image and extreme sensitivity to the opinions of others. However, the psychiatrist did nothing about these important issues. Four months later, Claire attended me in a state. Sedated on the medication, she could not function properly. Over the next few weeks, I weaned her off all medication. She felt a lot better off medication. I then referred her and her family to a psychotherapist. Three years later, she has finished school and created an independent life for herself.

In an article on depressive illness in the elderly in the *Irish Medical News* of 20 March 2000, psychiatrist Dr Ciaran Corcoran wrote that elderly people in nursing homes are particularly at risk of depression. By way of an explanation, he stated that these elderly patients were more likely to have physical problems or dementia. Yet there are other obvious reasons why the elderly in nursing homes are more likely to become depressed. They have been removed from their home and familiar surroundings. They may be separated from family and loved ones, and in some nursing homes at least, patients have little to do to occupy their time. In my opinion, the medical profession's downplaying of emotional, psychological and social causes of depression in comparison to physical causes is a serious oversight.

QUESTIONING THE MEDICAL VIEW

Most doctors conduct their consultations with clear understanding that the doctor is the expert. The doctor will tell the patient what is wrong with him and what treatment he needs, because doctor knows best. He listens to the patient all right, but as he listens, he is preoccupied by what he sees as his main priority in the consultation – to make a 'diagnosis' so he can commence 'treatment' – which usually means drug treatment.

The medical profession believes that antidepressant drugs are 70 per cent effective in treating depression. In 1980, when I was studying psychiatry in medical school, this 70 per cent cure rate was accepted as gospel – an established fact. Yet according to highly respected psychiatry textbooks at the time antidepressant drugs were first introduced (the late 1950s), depression had a spontaneous recovery rate of 70 to 80 per cent without *any* drug treatment.

Doctors believe that the case for using antidepressant drugs is very strong; 70 per cent effectiveness compared to 30 per cent using a placebo. Some medical experts – most notably *Toxic Psychiatry* author Dr Peter Breggin – are concerned that the research which has 'proved' that antidepressants are 70 per cent effective may not be nearly as reliable as the medical profession believes. In his book *Talking Back to Prozac*, Dr Breggin points out that, in the Prozac FDA trials, as many as between 30 and 50 per cent of people taking Prozac dropped out of the studies, either due to side effects or lack of effectiveness. A simple mathematical calculation shows that a 70 per cent improvement rate is impossible. Dr Breggin contacted one of these researchers, who claimed these studies demonstrated a 60 to 70 per cent success rate with Prozac. The researcher admitted to Dr Breggin that he did not include the one third of his patients who had dropped out of the study in his calculations. Including these study drop-outs – as they obviously should have been – only 47 per cent of people on Prozac improved – a far cry from a 70 per cent success rate.

Results from the 1999 study by Professor Malt – lauded by psychiatrists – do not support a 40 per cent difference in effectiveness between antidepressant drugs and placebo. Remission occurred in 47 per cent of patients who received the placebo, compared to 54 per cent with one antidepressant and 61 per cent for a second antidepressant. Medical research suggests that antidepressants are only 50 per cent effective in adolescents. This is barely distinguishable from the effects of placebo, and should raise serious questions about our approach to depression in young people.

Doctors believe that 70 per cent of suicides are the result of untreated or poorly treated depression. It should therefore be relatively easy to prove that antidepressants are as effective in reducing the suicide rate as they are in treating depression. Yet numerous studies have failed to prove that antidepressants reduce the suicide rate at all. Some research has indicated that these drugs may increase the likelihood of suicide. Nevertheless, the basic strategy in the medical profession's fight against suicide is to seek out and find everyone suffering from depression and put them on antidepressant medication.

JACK'S 'BREAKDOWN'

I had known Jack and his family for about four years. Married with four children, he always appeared relaxed and cheerful. One day he came to my surgery, very distressed and extremely anxious. 'Doctor, I think I'm cracking up,' he cried. Jack thought he was having a nervous breakdown. Earlier that day, stressed to breaking point, Jack had walked out of work without saying a word to anyone. He walked straight to a river and thought about ending it all. Thankfully, his strange behaviour was noticed by a passer-by who brought him home. In my surgery, he was distraught.

Jack thought he was losing his mind. He was keen to see a psychiatrist, so I arranged this for him. Over the next two weeks, the psychiatrist adopted one approach and I another. The psychiatrist quickly diagnosed that he was acutely depressed and prescribed antidepressant medication. Other than these tablets, the psychiatrist did not recommend any form of therapy. Jack's experience illustrates the differences between a typical psychiatric approach to human distress and an approach which focuses on listening and understanding. I asked Jack to write about this experience in his own words:

Looking back, I can't remember when I started to feel the way I did about myself. But I do know when it began to change for the better. I always thought I was easy-going, on top of things, cool and in control, at work, home and play. I know now that what I was actually doing was filling up my time with a lot of things to do so I would not have to think about myself or my fears. I always seemed to be worried about what others thought of me. I was preoccupied with doing things to make others happy. It did not seem to matter to me how I felt, so long as everyone else was happy.

I went into the career I have today because my father wanted me to have a trade, something he never had himself. I don't blame him. He was trying to give me a better standard of life. But I ended up spending nearly all my life working at something I never wanted to do. This kind of attitude – trying to please others – ran my life for a long time. I couldn't handle saying no. I just took everything on. I was afraid of letting my wife and kids down. I was always scared stiff that if I didn't bring home enough money every week to have a good standard of living, I would not be good enough for my wife.

I knew my wife loved me. But to keep this love, I felt I had to keep up to a certain standard, or else I was not good enough. I know now that if I had talked to her I would have found out sooner or later that she loved me for *me* and not for what we did or did not have in material terms. I thought people didn't care about how I felt. I stopped thinking about me and I pushed my own needs deep down inside myself. I hid my feelings away. I felt that I was coping, but denying my feelings made me feel bad and was eating me away inside. It all came to a head one day at work when one more small thing needed to be done, and only I could do it. Something just went 'STOP!': a sort of bang inside me.

I felt 'I just cannot do this. I can't keep going. I can't cope any more. I don't want to cope. I want to stop. I want to cry. I can't do this any more. If this is me I would be better off dead.' I just stormed straight out of work without a word to anyone and wandered off. I wandered around for hours. I am not sure how I felt – full of emotion, full of fear, pain, loss, full of dislike for myself. *Lost.* I did not know what to do. My emotions were taking me over. I was very afraid. I felt like a lost child. I wanted to hurt myself.

With encouragement from my wife, I went to see my doctor, Terry Lynch. I thought that a little medication would help to sort me out, help me relax for a while. Soon I'd get back on top of things like I was before. When I went to my doctor and said 'I can't cope', he really listened to what I was saying. This is when it all came out – a flood of emotions. It was overpowering. I began to see that I was living my life for others. Just talking about it and being listened to helped me. With my doctor's help, I began to learn about myself, who I *really* was. He helped me to see how low my self-esteem was. He encouraged me to like myself for who I am. He helped me to look at my life as if I was on the outside, looking in. This helped me to see the problem areas and also the good areas. He helped me to help myself to relax. He did not prescribe any medication.

During this time, I also went to see a psychiatrist. I initially felt he might be able to help me as well. Though he listened to what I was saying, he did not hear what I had to say. He said, 'You're a bit depressed' and prescribed some antidepressant drugs. The next time I went back to the psychiatrist, he was only interested in how the drugs were working. He said, 'It's depression, the drugs will work soon.' At my third visit to the psychiatrist, he again was only interested in the drugs. He seemed to get annoyed with me when I said that I wasn't finding the medication very helpful. He then (at my *third* visit!) decided to talk to me. He began with a lot of questions about my life and my childhood, my social habits, and so forth. From this, he concluded that I was depressed because I did not want to go to work.

He openly wondered if I might just be trying to get off sick from work for a few weeks. I found that very insulting. He just wasn't getting the message. I had, after all, felt so bad that I had considered taking my own life. He seemed to dismiss that. So I decided I was not going back to him again. Even that decision was an indicator that I was rebuilding my self-esteem! With the help of my own doctor, I began to relax. He encouraged me to like myself, to keep reminding myself that I am a very important and worthy person. He helped me to accept myself as I am. He worked very closely with me over a short period of time. He helped me to build confidence in myself as an individual.

As a result, I became stronger and stronger as a whole person. I never felt better in my life. After four to five weeks, I was ready to return to work, where I was soon able to use all I had learned about myself. I was now able to say 'No, I can't handle that at the moment' without feeling the shame of letting people down. I also made a decision to move to a less stressful job. One year later, I did just that, but that year proved to me just how strong I had become. All this happened five years ago and I have not looked back. Whatever happens now in my life, I know I can handle it.

Few GPs would have had the courage or the understanding to disagree so strongly with what the psychiatrist was doing. My doctor's stance gave me the courage to stand up to the psychiatrist rather than sit there and accept as gospel every word he said. I know that from hearing people talk about the treatment they and their loved ones receive from the doctors they go to.

My philosophy of life now is: 'believe in yourself, like yourself, and encourage yourself.'

I never believed that Jack was 'psychiatrically ill'. His self-esteem was very low, and he needed a great deal of approval from others, particularly from his colleagues at work. Jack was extremely self-critical. He constantly put himself under severe pressure to have everything just right, to be the best employee in the company. He wanted to say no when asked to do overtime or when more work was put his way than his fellow workers were being given. But he could not say no because he needed their approval so badly. He always said, 'Sure, I'll do it'.

For years he denied his true feelings, until the bubble burst. He walked out of his job and went to the river in a highly stressed state, eventually ending up in my surgery. Over the next two weeks, while the psychiatrist was diagnosing 'depression' and prescribing antidepressants, I worked with Jack on his self-esteem. I recommended tapes and books on personal growth and inner peace. Because I believed in Jack, I helped him believe in himself. Within two weeks, Jack had attended me five times, each consultation lasting over an hour. People in distress need a lot of time.

Jack was back at work within four to five weeks. He was calm, relaxed, only this time it wasn't a show. This time round he really was relaxed and at peace with himself. Jack stopped the antidepressants prescribed by the psychiatrist – who had said he would need them for nine months – within two weeks. He told me that he could not connect with the psychiatrist. They were on different wavelengths – how often I have heard patients say that about doctors!

We doctors are trained to respond as the psychiatrist did: seeking to diagnose and treat rather than to listen, understand and empower our patients. Had Jack attended another GP, it is likely that he would have been persuaded to take antidepressants for nine months. He probably would not have grown from his experience as he did. Jack had a healing, therapeutic relationship with me. Not so with his psychiatrist, despite attending him three to four times in two weeks.

Geraldine went through an emotional crisis, resulting in her being admitted to a psychiatric hospital for a month. After the admission, Geraldine worked hard to get her life back on track. She decided that it would be best for her to return to work a few weeks before Christmas. That way, she would have crossed that bridge before Christmas, and she would be able to relax during the holidays. Her psychiatrists were totally against this. They felt that Geraldine should stay off work for quite a while longer. She cried for hours after being told that. I could see that going back to work sooner rather than later was very important to Geraldine. Staying off any longer could be counter-productive to her recovery. I went against the views of the psychiatrists and certified her fit for work three weeks before Christmas. Since then, Geraldine's recovery has continued steadily, and she has been back at work without any problems for the past six months. Just as they tend to overestimate the value of medication, many doctors underestimate the importance of social reintegration in the healing process. When people are trying to rebuild their sense of self-belief, it greatly helps if they sense that their carers believe in them.

A Person or an Object?

American Carl Rogers was a leading therapist of the twentieth century. He pioneered an approach to therapy based upon deep respect for the client, now widely known as client-centred therapy. Irvin Yalom MD, professor emeritus of psychiatry at Stanford University School of Medicine, wrote the introduction to Rogers's book, *A Way of Being*. The following passage from Yalom's introduction demonstrated Rogers's passionate belief that clients must be treated as human beings with great respect and dignity:

> At an academic symposium on Ellen West, a heavily studied patient who committed suicide several decades before, Rogers startled the audience by the depth and intensity of his reaction. Not only did Rogers express his sorrow at her tragically wasted life, but also his anger at her physicians and psychiatrists who, through their impersonality and preoccupation with precise diagnosis, had transformed her into an object. How could they have? Rogers asked. If only they had known that treating a person as an object always stands

in the way of successful therapy. If only they had related to her as a person, risked themselves, experienced her reality and her world, they might have dissolved her lethal loneliness.

As mainstream medicine becomes increasingly biological in its approach to human beings, the impersonal approach alluded to by Carl Rogers is becoming increasingly prevalent. When Helen became depressed in her early forties, she sought help from her GP, who quickly informed her that her depression was caused by a biochemical brain abnormality. That doctor's impersonal clinical approach did little for Helen. She subsequently attended me, and I asked her to write about the effect that GP consultation had on her:

It is very traumatic to be labelled with the term 'depression' five minutes after walking into the doctor's surgery, especially when you have no idea what is happening to you. The term is dished out in a matter-of-fact way without compassion or understanding – an empty, meaningless word that strikes terror into the heart and brings horrible images to the mind. The patient is then left to deal with it on their own.

I believe it is not psychiatric theory or diagnosis that will help a person. Rather, it is knowing and feeling that somebody is there for you at a truly human level. That you can talk to that person and know that you are not being judged or labelled. A depressed person will never open up fully to a person whom they suspect is just waiting to categorise them further like an inanimate object – I wouldn't open up, anyhow.

Depressed people have received too many negative labels either directly or indirectly throughout their lives. Further negative messages are very detrimental to the image they have of themselves, especially when they are given by a psychiatrist or GP who is not prepared to nurture them in a caring relationship. I can only see the medical profession's approach of psychiatric diagnosis and tablet prescribing as adding to the feelings of worthlessness and isolation being experienced by the depressed patient. What people need most is just to be listened to and to know they are being listened to.

Labelling a person with 'clinical depression' and telling them it is caused by a biochemical imbalance or genetic defect is as traumatic as telling a person they have a terminal illness. The medical profession must wake up to this and realise what they are doing. Doctors have the power in their hands to wreck people's lives. People with depression who contemplate suicide do not have a psychiatric disorder. Depression is not a 'disorder' – it is a range of very strong overwhelming feelings. Surely feelings are not disorders or abnormalities. Psychiatrists take people's power away from them with such statements.

The most difficult part of the depression for me is the feeling of loneliness and loss. I know this is a feeling and I know I've got to listen to it and understand it. If the medical profession label that as being mentally ill, well then the whole of humanity is mentally ill, because every human being is a feeling being. Some of us feel more than others. We are made to feel guilty for this and we are labelled for it. Do the research studies which these 'experts' carry out investigate the amount of pain and rejection depressed people had experienced in their lives even when they tried to bring love to people in their lives who hurt them? Of course not! That would require too much compassion, under-standing and time! Better to write us all off as being the same – hopeless medical cases – all our lives explained away by a magical convenient medical abnormality that we were all unfortunate enough to develop. How tidy!

In my opinion, a person's greatest need is to belong. When you don't feel you belong anywhere you are lost. When you feel you don't even belong to yourself, you feel a huge loss and despair. When you are lost to yourself, then who can pull you through? Who is left? Of course these feelings cause despair. You will think of any way out, including suicide. That is your protection. It is the one control that you have after so much has been taken away from you – and you won't let go of that. I don't think you are mentally ill because you choose to cling to that one part of you that you still have power over.

Antidepressant drugs cannot combat the pain I feel inside. No tablet will heal what I've seen at home growing up – alcohol abuse, extreme violence, terror, pain, silent resignation. I am stronger in ways because of my life experiences but very damaged too. It is the internalisation of the painful feelings from these experiences and the burial of these emotions into the most private areas of your being that probably sets the seeds for the loneliness of depression. You knew that loneliness at the time of the painful and terrifying experiences in childhood – but only for a split-second, because that is all the pain you could cope with at the time. I took antidepressants which were prescribed for me. They made me feel far worse – weird and spaced out. I came very close to heading for the river while I was on them.

The medical profession would do well to take note of Helen's comments. Thousands of people have had the same experience at their hands. One of psychiatry's current aims is to de-stigmatise psychiatric illness. But the stigma of mental illness is there largely because of psychiatry. I cannot see how the stigma of mental illness can be removed when these same experts tell us that so-called 'psychiatric illnesses' are caused by biochemical abnormalities, particularly when there is no conclusive evidence to prove this.

The judgements the public make about depression and other so-called 'psychiatric illnesses' stem largely from how society sees 'psychiatric illness' which in turn is created by how psychiatry views these 'illnesses'. To remove the stigma, the public need to receive a different message about 'mental illnesses': that they are a sane and understandable human reaction to deep emotional hurts. It took Helen months to recover from the stigma she felt when her GP told her that her depression was caused by a biochemical brain defect.

DEPRESSION: A WITHDRAWAL WITHIN

Depression is an understandable withdrawal reaction in a person who has experienced an overwhelming degree of emotional pain. I believe that in the case of every person who develops depression – including people with severe depression for which psychiatry has been unable to find a cause – there is always a reason. The reason can be understood in the following context. In order to defend fundamental human emotional needs – to feel safe and secure, to avoid being hurt – the person reacts by protecting themselves when feeling threatened. People who become depressed protect themselves by withdrawing from people and from life. Reaching out, taking risks and interacting with others has become too risky, for fear of further rejection.

The severity of the depression depends on how threatened the person feels and how much they need to withdraw. This can vary greatly. For some people, the depth of the pain of depression is indescribable. I believe that people do not deliberately choose to become depressed. It is a sub-conscious response, the only way the person can defend himself from further rejection, hurt or humiliation. Depression can occur when a person finds themselves in a difficult, stressful situation, particularly when all possible solutions seem excruciatingly painful or threatening. As if paralysed by the enormity of their pain and the seeming impossibility of an acceptable resolution, the person withdraws and becomes depressed. Depression can sometimes be a protective mechanism to avoid experiencing feelings that terrify the person, such as feelings of severe anxiety; fear of emotional annihilation; rage or other feelings for which there seems to be no outlet, no resolution. It is inaccurate to label emotionally vulnerable people who have a strong need to protect themselves by withdrawing as 'mentally ill' and suffering from 'abnormal brain biochemistry'. The following two case stories illustrate the link between depression and the need to withdraw from life. They also demonstrate how important life events are as a trigger for depression.

Alice's Story

Alice was happily married with three children. She had a good relationship with her husband. A row with their neighbours escalated out of all proportion and ended up in court. Alice had no previous history of depression or emotional distress, but all that changed coming up to the court case. Unable to face life, Alice began to withdraw, spending most of the day in bed. She lost interest in her work and her family. Alice spent most of her day crying. She felt very depressed and saw no point in living any more. She was distraught when she came to see me. The court case was the following week.

Alice cried and sobbed her way through the consult-ation. Throughout our meeting, I kept referring back to her uniqueness as a human being and suggesting that it was possible for her to separate her true value as a unique human being from what was going to happen in the courts. I gave her ample time to express herself, to get it all out. Alice felt a good deal better after our meeting, having released pent-up emotion in a safe and supportive environment. She left, not with a prescription, but with a new-found sense of energy and awareness of her self-worth. Our meeting helped Alice put things in perspective, not because I made a diagnosis and put her on drug treatment or because I told her where she was going wrong. That consultation worked well because I did not judge or criticise her. From the outset, I sought to convey to Alice that her feelings made sense. I listened intently to her. Alice did far more talking than I did.

She needed a lot of time that day. She spend one and a half hours with me. Extra time is often well spent, allowing the crisis to be thoroughly dealt with and reducing the need for future therapy sessions. Had she attended a different doctor, I believe – as does she – that they would have given her fifteen minutes and a prescription either for tranquil-lizers to calm her down or an antidepressant.

When I met Alice three months later, the court case was over. The dispute with her neighbours was settled. Her depression had disappeared. She was eagerly planning to redecorate her home. She told me that her consultation with me had helped enormously, giving her the en-couragement to face the court case.

Hilda's Story

Hilda was in her forties when she attended me. She complained of recurring depression and anxiety for over fifteen years. Hilda had attended psychiatrists and a psychologist. She had been diagnosed as having endogenous depression and had taken several different anti-depressants which had not helped her. For the previous five years, Hilda had been taking three tranquillizers and a sleeping tablet every day. Hilda believed that she was addicted to these drugs and felt angry about this. She could think of no reason why she had become depressed and anxious, but these feelings were ever-present in her life for years. She said that neither the psychologists nor the psychiatrists had come up with a reason for her depression.

After her second session with me, I felt I understood her depression, to some degree at least. Hilda had been quite anxious and insecure as a teenager. She coped well enough until her late twenties. Then, within ten months, she lost the three people who were closest to her. First her mother died suddenly. Hilda had always been very close to her mother. Next, her marriage broke up. A few months later, her only sister also died suddenly. In the space of ten months, the bottom had fallen out of Hilda's world. Her depression began soon after these losses. I believe that Hilda subconsciously reacted to these dreadful losses by withdrawing from people and from the world. At least by withdrawing and not reaching out, she would avoid the risk of repeating the awful pain and loneliness that came with feeling abandoned.

She paid a price for this withdrawal – no intimate

relationships in her life. But anything was better than the terrible pain of trusting and reaching out only to lose the people she trusted and reached out to. Five years after her marriage broke up, she entered another relationship. She had two sons with this partner and fifteen years later they are still together. This man has been wonderful for Hilda, but she has never been able to let down the barriers and really trust in this relationship. It is as if, twenty years ago, when her whole life fell apart, she decided she would never again risk experiencing such pain and abandonment.

This explanation for why she has been depressed for twenty years made sense to Hilda. For years it had been safer for her to stay where she was in her life than to take even tentative steps towards connecting with her partner and others. Medication could never be the solution she needed. Yet the psychiatrists she had attended had prescribed several different drugs, none of which helped. Hilda was soon ready to deal with her suppressed emotional pain. She is now attending a counsellor to explore these issues.

I now believe that depression is not a 'psychiatric illness'. Depression is a coping mechanism, a withdrawal within oneself when reaching out to others has become too painful, too risky. Depression is an unhappy place to be, but for the person who suffers with it, depression is the lesser of two evils. An autumn 1998 study published in the *British Journal of General Practice* suggested that depression is more likely in people exhibiting certain characteristics. The researchers from Leeds University spent fifteen years following the lives of more than 130 GPs. The researchers found that the GPs who as medical students experienced depression, high self-criticism, sibling rivalry and/or excessive alcohol intake were more likely to develop a serious depression later in life. The results also suggested that having difficult relationships within the family of origin increased the likelihood of difficult relationships with medical colleagues during their working life. This research does not support the hypothesis that depression is biological in origin.

Doctors believe that depression serves no purpose. We have had 'Fight Depression' and 'Defeat Depression' campaigns, as if depression were an enemy to be exterminated. These campaigns have received great publicity. But they have made little impression, either on depression or on the suicide rate. I believe that even the most severe depressions make sense, and are understandable in the context of the life that person has lived and experienced.

The process of withdrawal frequently begins many years earlier, gradually escalating to the degree of withdrawal which is labelled 'mental illness'. When Jill attended me in her mid-twenties with depression, she recalled feeling like an outsider throughout her school days. In national school from the age of five upwards, Jill remembers being separate from the rest of her classmates. She was too timid to get involved in the everyday games and play, regularly standing alone by the yard wall, watching the others play. This pattern of withdrawal and timidity gradually escalated, unnoticed by family and teachers alike, until eventually it reached the point where she was diagnosed as having depression.

James, also in his twenties, attended me with so-called 'social phobia'. He became extremely nervous when in company, and as a result avoided social contact as much as possible. As we explored his life story, he recounted having recently seen a video of his first communion. While all the other first-time communicants were happily running all over the place with excitement, he noticed that he did not leave his parents' side throughout the day. James recalled feeling scared and intimidated and staying beside his parents in an unsuccessful effort to feel safe and secure. Quiet children, like Jill and James, often slip through the net. Because they don't draw attention to themselves, and they are compliant at school, their anguish can easily go unnoticed.

'BUT DOCTOR, WHERE DOES MY DEPRESSION GO EVERY WEDNESDAY?'

Joan had experienced severe anxiety for over a year. It was dominating her life. One evening she felt so stressed that she visited her doctor about it. The GP was certainly conscientious – he spent almost an hour with her. Most of that hour consisted of a ping-pong match between Joan and the GP about whether or not she should take medication for her anxiety. The GP concluded that Joan's anxiety was a symptom of depression. The doctor spent a great deal of time explaining the prevailing medical view about depression to Joan: that it is caused by a brain imbalance which is corrected by taking antidepressant drugs.

The GP was insistent. He wanted Joan to take antidepressants. Joan wanted help with her anxiety but was not convinced that an antidepressant drug was what she needed. Exasperated, Joan said, 'If my depression is caused by a biochemical brain imbalance, then where does my depression go every Wednesday, Doctor?' The GP stopped in his tracks. 'What do you mean?' he asked. Joan repeated, 'If my depression is due to a biochemical brain imbalance, why am I never depressed on Wednesdays?' The doctor asked Joan if there was something she did on Wednesdays that made her feel better.

Joan already knew the answer to her own question. Every Wednesday, she attended a counsellor, who was based quite a distance from Joan's home. So on Wednesday, most of Joan's day was spent preparing for the consultation (which she eagerly looked forward to every week), travelling to the counsellor, and home again. Joan explained all this to the GP, who was still unable to explain why she did not experience depression on Wednesdays. Joan then explained to the doctor why she did not feel depressed on the days she visited her therapist. She had a wonderful relationship with her counsellor. That hour every week was like gold to her. She felt safe, she felt loved every Wednesday, so she did not feel depressed. The doctor admitted that her version made sense.

Little wonder that the GP was knocked off his stride. In one fell swoop, Joan – a mere patient – exploded the medical profession's fondly held theory about depression being caused by a biochemical imbalance. How could a biochemical imbalance revert to normal on Wednesdays and suddenly become abnormal again the next day? He had no answer to her common sense. In fairness to the GP, at the end of the consultation he said to Joan that they had both learned something. He was half-right. *He* had certainly learned something. Joan was the teacher; the doctor was the pupil.

POST-NATAL DEPRESSION

Depression is relatively common after childbirth. The prevailing view within the medical profession is that post-natal depression is a biological disorder, requiring treatment with antidepressant drugs. Consequently, the personal, social and relationship changes a woman goes through during and after childbirth receive inadequate recognition from the medical profession. Post-natal depression is sometimes attributed to the hormonal changes which accompany childbirth. While there may be a biological element to post-natal depression, this possibility has not been proven and remains purely speculative. But the emotional upheaval associated with childbirth is not speculative; it is a fact of life.

Suddenly the woman finds herself responsible for a helpless infant. Her life has changed forever. As if life wasn't busy enough already, this tiny creature will need feeding, clothing and minding for the next twenty years, and the buck stops with her. Her relationships – with herself, her partner, her whole world – have irrevocably changed. Her plans for her own life have to be put on hold. While the joys of new motherhood are well recognised in society, the stresses are not. Some women find themselves with very little support. They have to cope more or less alone.

Caring for her own baby may trigger memories and emotions of the mother's own childhood. If as a child she experienced a great deal of loneliness and sadness, these emotions may come flooding back as she cares for her own child. A woman who has been barely coping with life may find childbirth and motherhood overwhelming. Subconsciously withdrawing into depression may be the only way the woman can avoid being overwhelmed by this new situation in which she finds herself.

A psychologist told me the following case history. A woman became severely depressed after childbirth. She had all the treatments psychiatry could offer, including antidepressants and admission to a psychiatric hospital. Her depression did not improve. As a last resort, the woman was referred to this psychologist. The root of the woman's depression remained elusive. The breakthrough came when the psychologist asked the woman at what times she felt most depressed. She replied, 'When I'm brushing my baby's hair'. It emerged that brushing her daughter's hair sparked off memories of her own childhood: memories of sadness, of feeling unloved. Her intense love for her child reminded her of how unloved she felt when she was growing up. These painful memories were at the root of her depression. In the ensuing months, she worked with the psychologist to explore and come to terms with her emotional pain. In the process, she overcame her depression.

What women with post-natal depression need is social, emotional and psychological support. Post-natal depression is not a 'mental illness'. It is an understandable human response to one of the most challenging human experiences of all – becoming a mother. Why do we need psychiatric reasons when there is a perfectly adequate human explanation?

ANTIDEPRESSANTS

The term 'antidepressants' is a misnomer. It suggests that antidepressant drugs have been proven to act specifically against depression and that is not true. In the *Journal of the Royal Society of Medicine* in 1998, Bruce Charlton MD recommended that antidepressants should be made available on request. He believes that antidepressants will help people who are not depressed to feel 'better than well'. He is, in effect, saying that life is tough, so why not take antidepressants if they make you feel better, even if you are just frustrated or unhappy?

That antidepressants make non-depressed people feel better demonstrates that these drugs are not specifically antidepressant in their action. This supports my belief that these drugs act as non-specific stimulant drugs.

Initially I was shocked by what seemed a lack of any scientific perspective on the use of antidepressants in Dr Charlton's article. Then I realised that he is merely describing current trends in medical practice. Antidepressants have become so widely prescribed that all a person has to do is to show signs of emotional distress, which is then interpreted by doctors as depression. In his annual report published in 1998, Sir Kenneth Calman, Chief Medical Officer for England, noted the sharp rise in the prescribing of antidepressants. He indicated that in the previous two years, prescriptions for antidepressant drugs had risen by 15 per cent in men and 19 per cent in women. He noted that one in twelve women and one in twenty-eight men were prescribed these drugs, and the prevailing medical view is that many more people should be taking them.

Although the older antidepressants (many of which are still widely used) have been on the market for over forty years, the medical profession has never established how they work. The only thing which can be said with any certainty about the older antidepressants is that they certainly do tend to sedate. If they do make people feel better, the sedation may well be the reason. As psychiatrist Dr Peter Leyburn wrote in *The Lancet* of 25 November 1967, twelve years after these drugs were first introduced, 'it is difficult to feel depressed when you are unconscious.'

Nor do doctors understand how newer antidepressants such as Prozac or Seroxat work, though this is not the impression one gets when medical experts speak in the media. Doctors convey a message to the public that the profession does understand how these drugs work. In the case of the majority of these newer antidepressant drugs, the profession believes they act by rebalancing the levels of serotonin or other chemicals in the brain. This is guesswork, since no proof exists that depression is caused by an imbalance of either serotonin or any other brain chemical. Nor is there any conclusive evidence that antidepressants have a balancing effect on the level of any chemicals in the brain.

Certainly some people who take these newer anti-depressants do feel better. Many people get a buzz, a sense of energy from these drugs. For a person who has had neither a buzz nor a sense of energy for quite some time, this can be a most welcome development. But this does not mean that these drugs work to counteract a specific – and as yet unproven – chemical imbalance in the brain.

Many people feel worse when they take the newer antidepressant drugs. In many cases, symptoms such as anxiety, agitation, insomnia and unreality are heightened. Just as the only statement regarding how the older antidepressants work which can be made with any certainty is that they sedate, the only thing which can be said with confidence about how the newer antidepressants act is that they tend to stimulate.

Side effects of Prozac which point to its stimulant effect include fever, nausea, diarrhoea, loss of appetite, nervousness, insomnia, anxiety, tremor, dizziness, convulsions, hallucinations, psychosis, hypomania and mania. The majority of the listed side effects of Favarin, another newer antidepressant, are also typical of an excessive stimulation of the body and the nervous system: nausea, vomiting, diarrhoea, palpitations, sweating, anorexia, anxiety, tremor, agitation, insomnia, dizziness and convulsions.

While the medical profession and the pharmaceutical industry go to great lengths to convince people that antidepressants are not addictive, the public are reluctant to accept this. A British MORI survey in 1995 revealed that 78 per cent of those interviewed believed that antidepressants are addictive. Only 16 per cent thought that people with depression should be offered antidepressants. But 91 per cent said that counselling should be available to depressed people. Could it be that people instinctively know what is good for them and what is not?

Most doctors remain convinced that antidepressants are not addictive. With great authority, in public and in consultations with patients, doctors repeat over and over again that there is no risk of addiction with antidepressant drugs. The public are not convinced. I believe the public are right to be concerned, given that virtually every medication prescribed by the medical profession for emotional distress has turned out to be addictive, ineffective, or likely to cause major side effects.

For many years – before the newer antidepressants such as Prozac were on the market – psychiatrists claimed that many people with depression were not being adequately treated by GPs because the prescribed dosage was too low. Prozac, launched in the late 1980s, has been widely prescribed for over ten years, as have several other newer antidepressants. Like many of the newer antidepressants, Prozac was initially marketed as a one-dose-strength antidepressant. The vast majority of people taking Prozac were prescribed the recommended dose of one 20-milligram tablet a day. The risk of prescribing an inadequate dose of Prozac and other newer antidepressant drugs had apparently been eliminated. Yet Prozac has not been shown to be any more effective than the older antidepressants.

In recent years, in my opinion because the initial buzz people feel from Prozac wears off within a few months, doctors have been increasing the dosage of Prozac. Now many people are prescribed four times the dosage of Prozac recommended just a few years ago. I believe that there are parallels here with drug addiction. On the Antidepressant Web discussion forum, many patients describe their experience of steadily having their dose of Prozac or other antidepressants increased. With each increase, the buzz returns for a short period, then fades.

As Charles Medawar points out, this need to increase the dose repeatedly to get that buzz raises to possibility that these people have actually become addicted to the drug.

It seems contradictory that Prozac is being used to treat one so-called 'psychiatric illness' yet it can precipitate four states which are themselves considered to be evidence of psychiatric illness – hallucinations, psychosis, hypomania and mania. A fifth serious side-effect of Prozac – convulsions – is itself a medical condition, for which long-term medical treatment is usually recommended. Prozac has also been implicated as a possible cause of suicide and of violent outbursts, including murder. The huge drive from the medical profession towards the wider prescribing of antidepressant drugs is based, not on scientific proof that they work, but on a combination of faith and wishful thinking.

Sometimes the drug companies who manufacture antidepressants are economical with the truth. One explanatory leaflet produced by Dista, the manufacturers of Prozac, states that Prozac and related drugs work by 'restoring the balance of serotonin in the brain'. I believe that this is an attempt to create the impression that the medical profession and the pharmaceutical industry know precisely what they are doing when they prescribe these drugs. The reality is that how Prozac 'works' has not been determined. Yet this statement appears on an information leaflet for the public as if it were an established fact. If Prozac worked by restoring the balance of serotonin in the brain, why would people who are *not* depressed experience similar effects with Prozac as depressed people? One of the few established actions of Prozac and similar drugs is that they do inhibit the reuptake of serotonin, an important brain chemical, hence the name SSRIs (Selective Serotonin Reuptake Inhibitors) for this group of drugs. However, there is no evidence that this action ameliorates depression. As it is a highly complex organ, the brain may well attempt to compensate for any such interference by becoming less sensitive to serotonin release in the brain. Since serotonin is present throughout most parts of the brain, interfering with the normal functioning of this chemical could have far-reaching consequences.

Any drug which stimulates the nervous system, which gives people an energy buzz, has the potential to be addictive. Many people who take the newer antidepressants find that when they stop taking them, their symptoms return. Their depression has not been cured, just masked by a stimulant drug. Doctors accept that many people who come off the newer antidepressants experience a withdrawal reaction.

In the 1970s and 1980s, the medical profession collectively made a major error of judgement regarding tranquillizers such as Valium, Ativan, and diazepam. Thousands of people reported to their doctors that when they discontinued these tranquillizers, their symptoms returned, often with a vengeance. Doctors decided that this occurred because the condition for which these drugs had been prescribed had not yet been cured. The patients needed a longer period of treatment. The real reason for the recurrence of symptoms was subsequently found to be a withdrawal reaction from an addictive drug. The medical profession's reluctance for years to admit that these tranquillizers were addictive resulted in the creation of millions of addiction problems. This would not have occurred had the medical profession heeded the warning signs.

I believe there is a real possibility that in the case of the newer antidepressant drugs, the medical profession is making precisely the same error of judgement all over again. Meanwhile, the underlying emotional distress which brought the person to the doctor in the first place remains unexplored and unresolved. Many patients who first attended the doctor with one problem – emotional distress – end up with two – their original emotional distress plus an addiction to medication.

It seems unrealistic to expect a drug to 'cure' the powerful emotions which a person with depression experiences. These feelings are of loneliness; a deep desire to reach out and talk to somebody but being afraid to do so; confusion; reduced concentration; indescribable feelings of grief and loss; panic; self-hatred; feeling useless and totally unworthy of love; immense feelings of inferiority sometimes to the point of feeling sub-human; emptiness; feelings of having already died; beliefs and value systems crushed; illusions of family relation-ships shattered; constant questioning of the purpose of life and searching for new meaning. It is even more unrealistic to expect drugs to cure these symptoms when doctors do not know how antidepressant drugs 'work'.

Prozac has been the largest selling antidepressant worldwide for several years. The public understandably presumes that this drug was tested and scrutinised thoroughly and with great care before it was made publicly available. Not so. According to Charles Medawar

in the Antidepressant Web, The US Food and Drug Administration's (FDA) testing of Prozac was far from
thorough and scientific. The FDA licensed Prozac on the
evidence of four trials. In three of these trials, patients
were allowed to take other mood-altering drugs (such as
tranquillizers) at the same time as they were taking
Prozac.

How can the effectiveness of one mood-altering drug be
properly and scientifically assessed when many patients in
the trial are taking other mood-altering drugs, and this fact
is not taken into account in the final results? The fourth
trial – the only one where patients taking other mood-
altering drugs were excluded from the trial – showed that
Prozac was no more effective than a sugar-pill.

According to the US label for Prozac – the official
American prescribing reference document – in 1996, eight
years after Prozac was first made available to the public,
neither the safety nor the effectiveness of Prozac has been
tested for use in in-patient depressive patients, or for
treatment of more than five to six weeks duration.

> The efficacy of Prozac was established in five-
> and six-week trials with depressed out-
> patients... the antidepressant action of Prozac
> in hospitalised depressed people has not been
> adequately studied... The effectiveness of
> Prozac in long-term use, that is, for more than
> five to six weeks, has not been systematically
> evaluated in controlled trials.
>
> (Lilly, 1996)

Yet this drug is widely prescribed for all three categories. The standard recommendation for a course of anti-depressant drugs is six to nine months. Once the FDA licences a drug, there is no comprehensive procedure in place to scrutinise how safe the drug is in the months and years after it goes on the market. According to the manufacturer's literature in 1996, eight years after its release, the possibility that Prozac might cause dependence or addiction had not been systematically studied.

The medical management of a depressed person has been reduced to deciding which medication, what dosage, and for what duration the medication should be prescribed. Rarely do doctors take other factors – such as the life experiences of the person – sufficiently into account. When doctors decide to stop antidepressant treatment, where stands the biochemical abnormality? Is it still there or has it been reversed by the antidepressant? Doctors have no idea. No tests will be done to assess the bio-chemical status of the person because no such tests exist.

Antidepressants are increasingly being prescribed for other 'conditions' such as social phobia and eating disorders. When Paula attended me for help with her social phobia, she had already attended a psychiatrist whose only treatment was to prescribe Prozac for three months. This did not help because it was not what Paula needed. Paula's core issues – such as her need to protect herself from hurt by staying away from people – were ignored by the psychiatrist. Like Paula, many people are caught in an emotional tug-of-war. On the one hand, they desperately want to socialise and have a full life. But on the other hand, deep insecurity, low self-esteem and fear paralyses them into inaction. Making progress entails working with the delicate dance between these two positions.

I have often heard doctors say in the media that the success rate of antidepressant treatment is 70 per cent. What is rarely stated is that the risk of a subsequent episode of major depression following nine months of antidepressant therapy is as high as 50 per cent. Nor is it said that with a second episode of depression, the risk of relapse following nine months of antidepressant treatment is 80 per cent. These figures are hardly consistent with the message being propagated by the medical profession: that antidepressants are a highly successful form of therapy. But this misguided message has got through to the public. For example, an article on depression in the *Irish Independent* of 6 May 2000 stated that '80 to 90 per cent of depressants, with proper treatment, achieve complete remission and lead successful, happy lives'. A minority of doctors do refer patients for counselling and psychotherapy. But the reality is that the vast majority of people who are diagnosed as having a 'mental illness' receive only drug treatment.

The medical profession's preoccupation with antidepressants in the treatment of depression means that few other options are considered. We could do with more imagination, more lateral thinking in medicine. Jemima Nielson outlined her experience of depression in the *Irish Independent* of 22 April 2000. She had been depressed since childhood, and after her grandmother died when she was sixteen years old, Jemima became anorexic. When aged twenty, suicidal although on antidepressants, Jemima went swimming with dolphins in Dingle Bay. She swam and frolicked with Fungi, Dingle's most famous tourist attraction. Her connection with Fungi changed her life. She immediately felt an immense calm. She felt an enormous sense of love from Fungi. She started playing with him. All the emotions she had kept bottled up poured out in that magical connection between human and dolphin. This was the turning point in her life. She soon came off antidepressants, felt less socially isolated and completed her university degree. Thirteen years later, she is happily married with two children.

I have never heard any prominent psychiatrist con-template the idea that dolphins may be worth researching in the treatment of depression. But perhaps dolphins and other natural life experiences could have significant therapeutic effects on people, as happened with Jemima.

4

OTHER 'MENTAL ILLNESSES'

Deciding that a symptom or a human behaviour is evidence of 'mental illness' is an arbitrary decision, a form of moral judgement. Homosexuality used to be considered a 'mental illness'. But now, within the diversity of modern society, people are demanding more freedom to express themselves sexually. Consequently, homosexuality is no longer believed to be a 'mental illness'. Similarly, 'mental illnesses' are diagnosed when a person exhibits characteristics which are judged by society to be abnormal. Society has decided that it is not normal or permissible to hear voices, to become seriously depressed, to become elated, to want to kill yourself. Rather than pigeon-hole the 'abnormality' (and consequently the person) into the appropriate diagnostic box, perhaps we should be asking ourselves if the boxes themselves need to be re-examined.

SCHIZOPHRENIA
Approximately 1 per cent of the population develops schizophrenia, amounting to about 36,000 people in Ireland. Schizophrenia accounts for 15 per cent of suicides. Almost

half of those with schizophrenia attempt suicide. One in ten succeed in ending their own life. Most psychiatrists and GPs believe that schizophrenia is a chronic brain disease. The medical consensus is that the hallucinations, delusions and other symptoms of schizophrenia are so bizarre that they must be caused by a brain abnormality of some kind. When speaking in public about schizophrenia, medical experts usually present an upbeat message. They outline how the medical profession now know that schizophrenia is a brain disease, a 'mental illness'.

When describing schizophrenia, psychiatrists frequently compare it to diabetes or other medical conditions. But to compare diabetes with schizophrenia is misleading for several reasons. It has been established that diabetes is due to an insulin deficiency. No biochemical or other physical defect has been identified in schizophrenia. Treatment for diabetes involves daily replacement therapy of insulin, the exact compound which is lacking in the body of the diabetic. Insulin in correct dosage can be used for a lifetime without risk of serious side effects.

Schizophrenia is treated with drugs for which no precise brain biochemical action has been established, and which frequently cause serious side effects that can be irreversible even when the drugs are stopped.

Behind the united public image psychiatrists portray there is a great deal of uncertainty and confusion about schizophrenia within psychiatry. This is illustrated in the *Oxford Textbook of Psychiatry*, third edition, 1996:

Of all the major psychiatric syndromes, schizophrenia is much the most difficult to define and describe. The main reason for this difficulty is that over the past 100 years, many widely divergent concepts of schizophrenia have been held in different countries and by different psychiatrists. Radical differences of opinion persist to the present day.

This textbook states that a diagnosis of schizophrenia in one country might well be diagnosed as depression in another:

> In New York, the concept [of schizophrenia] included cases that were diagnosed as depressive illness, mania, or personality disorder in the United Kingdom.

Dr Peter Breggin does not believe that schizophrenia is a mental illness. In *Toxic Psychiatry* he writes:

> Is there any such thing as schizophrenia? Yes and no. Yes, there are people who think irrationally at times and who attribute their problems to seemingly inappropriate causes, such as extraterrestrials or voices in the air. Yes, there are people who think they are God or the devil and repeat the claim no matter how much trouble it gets them into. But no, these people are not biologically defective or inherently different from the rest of us. They are not afflicted with a brain disorder or disease. They are undergoing a psychospiritual crisis, usually

surrounding basic issues of identity and shame, and typically with feelings of outrage and overwhelm.

They communicate in metaphors that often hint at the heart of their problems. The only reason to call them schizophrenic is to justify the psychiatric establishment and its treatments. By refusing to label people who already feel rejected and humiliated, we welcome them back to the human community and promote humane, respectful and loving attitudes towards them. And we help to prevent the rampant abuses we are documenting. Yet the reader has heard a whole different story in the press and on TV, and perhaps directly from psychiatrists: the story that schizophrenia is a genetic and biochemical disease subject to treatment with drugs.

Psychiatrist R. D. Laing expressed major reservations regarding the medical approach to schizophrenia in his book *Sanity, Madness and the Family* (1970):

Even two psychiatrists from the same medical school cannot agree on who is schizophrenic independently of each other in more than eight out of ten times at best; agreement is less than that between different schools, and less again between different countries. These figures are not in dispute. But when psychiatrists dispute the diagnosis, there is no court of appeal [for the patient]. There are at present no objective, reliable, quantifiable criteria – behavioural or neurophysiological or biochemical – to appeal to when psychiatrists differ. We [Laing and his co-workers] do not accept 'schizophrenia' as being a biochemical, neurophysiological, psychological fact, and we regard it as palpable error, in the present state of the evidence, to take it to be a fact.

Despite the prevalence of the diagnosis of schizophrenia (1 per cent of the population) there is no condition over which there is more dispute in the whole field of medicine. Every conceivable view is held by authoritative people as to whether 'schizophrenia' is a disease or a group of diseases; whether an identifiable organic pathology has been or can be expected to be found. There are no pathological anatomical findings at post-mortem. There are no organic structural changes noted in the course of the 'illness'. There are no physio-logical-pathological changes that can be correlated with these illnesses.

Mainstream psychiatry has ignored Laing's words of caution. The consensus view within psychiatry is that schizophrenia is a physical brain disease, although this presumption is not backed up by conclusive medical research. Yet the early warning signs of schizophrenia do not point to a physical problem. They clearly suggest that the central issue in schizophrenia is a major emotional crisis rather than a physical brain disease:

Early warning signs include social withdrawal, isolation, reclusiveness, suspiciousness of others, deterioration and abandonment of personal hygiene, flat emotions, inability to express joy, inability to cry or excessive crying, inappropriate laughter, excessive fatigue and sleepiness or an inability to sleep.

Schizophrenia Ireland information leaflet, 1998

Schizophrenia typically develops in the late teens and early twenties, a time of emotional upheaval and strained relationships within even the least dysfunctional families. The possibility that relationships within the family of a seriously emotionally disturbed person or stresses in their life might have contributed to the problem has not received enough attention from the medical profession. Most psychiatrists presume that, whatever may be causing this condition, it isn't pressures within the person's life. Yet some studies have shown a striking excess of major, stressful life events in the months prior to the onset of schizophrenia.

In *Sanity, Madness and the Family,* R. D. Laing described how he and his co-workers spent a great deal of time (twenty to forty hours in each case) with eleven patients diagnosed as having schizophrenia, and their families. They concluded that the symptoms which psychiatrists had labelled as bizarre and abnormal were understandable given the nature of the relationships within those eleven families.

I believe that schizophrenia is a consequence of deep insecurity and severe emotional turmoil. The person withdraws because life has become too terrifying. Hallucinations and delusions occur as an unconscious attempt to create meaning in life and to protect from further humiliation. Feeling totally unimportant, a young man becomes convinced he is someone very important – God, or a famous rock star. Feeling invisible, a young woman believes everyone is looking at her. Feeling that no one would be bothered talking to him, a person believes that they are being talked about on TV. Feeling too hurt and scared to interact with people socially, people with schizophrenia withdraw into isolation. The hallucinations and delusions create a fantasy world where the person is important and safe, to some degree at least. These hallucinations and delusions, often dismissed as meaningless by doctors, can have immense meaning for the sufferer. They typically revolve around issues of importance to all humans, but which become profoundly important for people struggling for their emotional survival: issues such as identity, the meaning of life and their life purpose. Who am I? Am I good and important (Jesus Christ, the Pope, a popstar or sportsperson) or am I evil or bad (the devil, smelly, a piece of dung). Do I matter, or am I invisible? Exploring the meaning of these symptoms with the person can be very productive.

Most psychiatrists believe that the 'thought disorder' experienced by people diagnosed as having schizophrenia is evidence of a breakdown in the brain's normal biochemical functioning. As with the other features of schizophrenia the prevailing medical view could be described in the following manner:

These features are so unusual that they must be caused by a physical defect in the brain. How could there possibly be any other explanation for such bizarre behaviour?

I am currently working with a young woman who has taught me a great deal about thought disorders. When I first met Alison, she had already been attending a psychiatrist for six months. Heavily sedated by the major tranquillizers prescribed by the psychiatrist, Alison appeared out of touch with what was going on around her.

Alison did not trust her psychiatrist. She felt that all he did was prescribe medication without listening to her. Alison never wanted the medication; she did not believe that drugs over a long-term basis would help sort out psychological problems. I knew that to make progress with Alison, I first had to create a trusting and respectful relationship with her. I set no goals for her. I concentrated on creating a relationship where Alison felt safe and not judged. Consequently Alison opened up to me far more then to her psychiatrist.

The psychiatrist repeatedly set targets for Alison. He insisted that she get up and go to bed at 'normal' hours. Each week he would set different goals which he expected Alison to achieve. Alison felt there was no way she could achieve these targets. Anyway, these goals did not seem that important to her at the time. Trying to understand what was going on within her seemed more important to her than what time she got up in the morning. The psychiatrist became frustrated with her failure to comply with his recovery plan. Consequently Alison learned to lie to the psychiatrist. She told him what he wanted to hear. By insisting that Alison follow his instructions, the psychiatrist inadvertently created a barrier between them. This gulf grew wider with each consultation.

Within weeks I felt that Alison would make little progress while taking such powerful drugs. Her thinking and speech were fuzzy from the medication. Fortunately, after six months of medication and getting nowhere, her psychiatrist acceded to Alison's request to reduce her medication. Three weeks later, tension was running high. Alison was spending hours – sometimes twenty-four hours – without moving, as if in a trance. Her parents were very worried and admission to a psychiatric hospital became a real possibility. By this time, Alison had finished with her psychiatrist. The psychiatrist's final recommendation to her was that she should now take Prozac. Alison and I wondered why, after six months taking major tranquillizers, the psychiatrist now saw fit to recommend Prozac, an entirely different category of drug. She declined the offer of Prozac.

Alison was locked into her thought pattern and could find no way out. Her parents were prepared to do anything to improve her condition, including hospitalisation if that would help, but I felt that the local psychiatric hospital would have little to offer except more medication. Alison, her parents and I came to an agreement. Alison would attend me twice a week for a fortnight. We would then arrange hospital admission if her condition remained unchanged.

The turning point came that week. Alison expressed a craving that someone would understand her current way of thinking. She had desperately wanted to discuss this with the psychiatrist, but she felt the psychiatrist did not want to know. Most psychiatrists view 'thought disorders' as crazy, purposeless thinking, confirming the diagnosis of schizophrenia. They do not see any point in exploring the person's thinking patterns. Satisfied that the person's thinking processes are different from 'normal' thinking, they switch to a consideration of what drug treatment would be appropriate. That week, Alison and I devoted two hours to an exploration of her thought processes.

When a thought came into her head, she felt a need to explore that thought to the nth degree. She would hold on to a thought in her mind until satisfied that she now understood every possible aspect of it. When other thoughts crept into her mind, as they naturally would, she tried to put them on hold until she had completed her work on the first thought. She then came back to the next thought and repeated the whole process. She could stay locked in this thinking process for hours on end, dealing with each thought queued up in designation order, thinking each thought through.

Her explanation made sense to me. Her 'thought dis-order' mirrored her current state of deep emotional in-security and fear. She had disassociated herself from life. The emotional turmoil she had experienced in recent years had shaken the foundations of her existence. She had nothing to hold on to, no anchor in the storm. Holding on to a thought for hours on end gave her a sense of control and safety which was missing in almost every other aspect of her life. She was hanging on to her thoughts for dear life. For hours she would not talk to her family. To talk would be to risk losing her train of thought. Alison felt that by losing her train of thought, she might literally be lost. She feared that she might then never be able to think straight again – what would she do then?

Alison felt that the medication really contributed to this dilemma, closing down her mind and her thought processes, increasing the fog, preventing her from connecting with happy memories, numbing the spark and inspiration she sought to guide her through this time. She had experienced insecurity in the years preceding her crisis and this insecurity suddenly escalated. She held the worry inside her, precipitating its growth and eventual climax. The medication blurred everything, reducing her ability to clear her head and to find inner peace. Alison felt that the major tranquillizing drugs disabled her brain and her thinking processes.

Alison was thrilled that her thinking patterns made sense to me. I had connected with her way of thinking. This had a profound effect on her, and it was a major turning point. Alison had found someone with whom she could discuss and explore her thinking processes. We discussed ways of letting go of this way of thinking. Among other things, I suggested that it was OK to let her thoughts come and go freely like clouds crossing the sky. I did not pressure her into changing her way of thinking. I reassured her that her need to hold on to her thoughts would diminish as her sense of inner safety and security increased. Her parents reported a major improvement during subsequent weeks. The possibility of hospital admission no longer arose. Alison is finding her feet again. She is back in full-time work, gradually reintegrating with life at her own pace, not mine – or the psychiatrist's.

We all become paranoid from time to time. The more vulnerable we feel, or the more we need to protect ourselves, the greater our paranoia. Some people become extremely paranoid, describing elaborate scenarios of being watched or followed. Because this paranoia appears groundless, doctors state that the person is experiencing delusions. It does not occur to them that, for the patient, the paranoia may be serving an important purpose.

A client of mine recently related the following story of her uncle's experience. The mother of the fifty-five-year-old man had just died. Desperately lonely, he visited his GP every week with a wide variety of symptoms. The GP concluded that he was schizophrenic and put him on anti-psychotic medication. The man quickly became very depressed, barely getting out of bed. This went on for months. Encouraged by his family, he consulted another doctor, who stopped his medication. The man soon returned to his old self. The medication prescribed for a condition from which he did not suffer sedated and depressed him so much that he could not function. What the man needed all along was human contact, to help him express and come to terms with the enormous grief he experienced when his mother died.

The human thinking process is very dynamic. We frequently experience more than a hundred thoughts a minute. Medical science does not know how thoughts are created. The biochemical activity which underpins the human thinking process has not yet been identified. No scientific basis exists which justifies the presumption that thought patterns such as Alison's are caused by abnormal brain biochemistry. Yet modern psychiatry presumes that this is the case.

Bertram Karon PhD and Anmarie Widener of the Psychology Research department at Michigan State University wrote on schizophrenia in the fall–winter 1999 edition of the *Ethical Human Sciences and Services* journal. They discuss the key role emotions play in the creation of schizophrenic symptoms:

> Eugen Bleuler (who first coined the term 'schizophrenia' in 1911) assumed wrongly that schizophrenics have no feelings. In fact, schizophrenic persons feel very intensely, although they may mask or even deny their feelings. The most basic affect is fear, actually terror. Human beings are not easily able to tolerate chronic terror. All of the symptoms of schizophrenia may be understood as manifestations of chronic terror and of defences against terror. Thus, withdrawal from people diminishes one's fear.
>
> The severity of the thought disorder varies with the severity of the terror. Chronic terror tends to mask other feelings. Nonetheless, the schizophrenic experiences – continuously or intermittently – anger, hopelessness, loneliness and humiliation. 'Inappropriate' affect is usually *socially* inappropriate, not inappropriate to the patient's inner experiences. We do not want to know about schizophrenia because we do not want to feel such intense terror. Given enough stress, any one of us may experience schizophrenic symptoms.

I recently met an old friend whom I had not seen for many years. As we reminisced, he spoke of Jim, a boy who grew up with us. My friend mentioned that Jim had been diagnosed as having schizophrenia in his twenties, and wondered about it as he pointed out that Jim had grown up in a happy home. But sometimes we do not know what is really going on in people's lives, within the four walls of home. I spent a lot more time in Jim's home than my friend, but I never felt comfortable there. The atmosphere in his home was usually tense, and the tension escalated greatly whenever his father was at home. When Jim was about eight years old, I recall seeing his mother on several occasions physically shoving food down his throat, roaring at him to eat his food. This terrified me, though at least I was secure in that it wasn't my throat which was being attacked. As a child of ten, Jim was anxious and very insecure; he had several behavioural problems, including daily bedwetting and soiling, for which he was again shouted at. His parents were pillars of the local community. Looking back now, I see that his parents were themselves highly stressed. They were doing their best, but they needed help and support. In his teenage years, Jim became very distressed, and was diagnosed as having schizophrenia. I do not think it was a coincidence that this boy who as a child was extremely insecure went on to be diagnosed with schizophrenia.

In January 2001 I attended a conference in Cork which marked the foundation of Cork Advocacy Network, a group seeking to give support and a voice to people diagnosed with 'mental illness'. One speaker, Paddy McGowan from Omagh, County Tyrone, spoke of how, after three years of contact with psychiatry and the mental health services, he told a psychiatric nurse about the voices he had been hearing for years, which to Paddy were as normal and familiar as the sun in the sky. The nurse sat up immediately, suddenly paying attention to his every word. The next day his diagnosis was changed from post-traumatic stress (precipitated by his experiences of working as a fireman during the Troubles in Northern Ireland, having to deal with the aftermath of shootings and bombings) to schizophrenia, and his whole life changed as a consequence. That happened in 1984, when he was twenty-three years old. It did not matter to the psychiatrists that he had heard voices for the previous fourteen years, and that to him they seemed entirely normal. Had the doctors explored the voices with him, they would have discovered that the voices began two weeks after the death of a much-loved relative, This surely pointed to a stress or grief reaction rather than evidence of a 'mental illness'.

Paddy was immediately put on major tranquillizers. He remained on this medication for ten years. Eventually, he decided that he was getting nowhere on this medication. With the help of friends who were themselves familiar with the process of weaning oneself off medication, he gradually came off the drugs. His final prescription would have knocked out a horse: Largactil, a major tranquillizer, 1,600mgs daily (300mgs is the highest recommended daily dose); Depixol, another major tranquillizer, injection of 80mgs weekly; Prothiaden, an antidepressant with sedative side effects, 150mgs twice daily (twice the highest recommended daily dose of 150mgs). Ironically, the only thing not tranquillized by this concoction of medication was the sound of the voices for which he was put on the medication in the first place.

Coming off the drugs in 1994 was a major struggle for Paddy, but he got through it. He hasn't looked back since. Apart from the group of people who helped him to come off the medication, Paddy did not tell anyone that he was coming off the drugs. Over the years he had learnt that if he did tell people (including the psychiatrists) they would insist that he continue with his medication. For three years, Paddy found himself in a bizarre situation: he was off all medication, but everyone around him thought he was continuing on the drugs as usual. Paddy's family and friends soon noticed big changes in him. They would often say that Paddy was 'himself' again. They marvelled at the wonders of modern medicine and in particular Paddy's medication, which was obviously now working effectively. Everyone was talking about the miraculous improvement in Paddy's condition. Paddy describes this as an 'internal prison'; he wanted to tell everyone that he was off medication and doing brilliantly without drugs, but he could not tell anyone, for fear of being persuaded (or even forced) to go back on his medication.

Paddy McGowan is writing his own book about his life and experiences. He has spoken at many conferences about his experiences and is currently involved in seeking reform of mental health services in Britain and Ireland.

A man called Peter attended me recently. Twenty-five years ago he was diagnosed as having schizophrenia. At the time, he was facing difficult examinations and couldn't cope with the strain. He has extensive experience of the psychiatric system. He had been on medication for the past twenty-five years. He told me he had learned to play the game, to be a 'good' patient, by doing what he was asked to do. He described his experience of how psychiatrists and nurses he encountered in hospitals kept their distance from the patients, handing out medication as if 'at the end of a forty-foot pole'. He told me that 'the psychiatric system closes you down, giving no springboard towards recovery and reintegration with society'. That was his experience of the psychiatric system.

A common belief among psychiatrists is that schizo-phrenia is a genetically inherited disorder. Irish psychiatrists Dr Conall Larkin and Abbie Lane expressed this belief in the *Irish Medical Times* in January 1998:

The most solid fact in terms of the cause of schizophrenia is that genetic factors play a role.

Having stated this 'solid fact', the authors seem to contradict this assertion in their very next sentence:

However, no clear pattern of (genetic) transmission has been identified.

Drugs have been the medical profession's treatment of choice for schizophrenia since the 1950s. Doctors still do not understand the mechanism of action of these drugs. Most medical researchers believe schizophrenia drugs work by changing the brain's chemistry in a beneficial way. The human brain is perhaps the most complex structure on this planet. There are billions of brain cells with an infinite number of possible interactions between them. Doctors do not understand the brain and how it functions. Yet most psychiatrists routinely prescribe these powerful drugs to their fellow human beings, not uncommonly for a lifetime.

The drugs most commonly prescribed for schizophrenia are the major tranquillizers, also known as anti-psychotic drugs. Increasingly psychiatrists favour the term 'anti-psychotic' in preference to 'major tranquillizer'. The reasons for this shift are worth looking at.

These drugs certainly are major tranquillizers. They have a far stronger sedative effect than the better known 'minor tranquillizers' such as Valium. But 'anti-psychotic' conveys the impression that these drugs have a specific anti-psychotic action, just as the word 'antidepressant' incorrectly suggests a specific antidepressant action. Describing these drugs as 'anti-psychotic' conveys a false impression of precision in their mode of action. This portrays modern psychiatric practice as a scientific specialty. But these major tranquillizers are not anti-psychotics. They are blunt instruments which induce sedation in most people, whether or not they have been diagnosed as schizophrenic. According to psychiatrists, anti-psychotic drugs are much better at suppressing symptoms such as agitation and restlessness than at surmounting the so-called 'negative' symptoms of schizophrenia: withdrawal or passivity, for example. But is this not disconcerting? Does this not suggest that these drugs act as major tranquillizers, tranquillizing the more active symptoms while having no effect on the 'negative' symptoms?

Bertram Karon and Anmarie Widener refer to this issue

in their aforementioned article:

> It was a public relations coup to relabel major tranquillizers as 'anti-psychotic medication', implying that they are as specific and as effective for psychosis as vitamin C is for scurvy. Unfortunately, there is no specific 'anti-psychotic' medication in that sense.

In September 1999, psychiatrist Dr Tom McMonagle wrote an article on the treatment of schizophrenia in the 'Advances in Psychiatry' supplement to the *Irish Medical Times*. He candidly expressed his concern about the effectiveness of medical interventions in schizophrenia:

> Between 1950 and 1998, over 2,000 randomised controlled trials have taken place on interventions for schizophrenia. These were surveyed by Adams at the Cochrane Schizophrenia Group in 1998 and his results must cause us to have reservations about the quality of data available for supporting clinical decisions. Nor is it correct to assume that the higher quality trials are necessarily the more recent ones. The combination of low numbers, massive drop-out rates, unrepresentative patients and short duration – the studies lasted an average of six weeks – make most of the trials irrelevant to everyday clinical practice.

It is worrying that drug treatments prescribed continuously for many years to millions of people worldwide have been tested in clinical trials only lasting an average of six weeks. Common sense suggests that six weeks is nowhere near long enough to assess the effectiveness and side-effect profile of a powerful mood-altering drug. Perhaps common sense is less common in medicine than it ought to be. A 1978 study in *International Pharmacopsychiatry* found that patients treated with placebo in hospital and no major tranquillizers on follow-up showed greater clinical improvement and less pathology at follow-up, fewer hospitalisations and less overall functional disturbance in the community. Only 8 per cent of those on no medication were readmitted, while between 43 and 73 per cent of those who received major tranquillizers were rehospitalised.

Dr Trevor Turner is a consultant psychiatrist at Homerton Hospital, London. He is a strong advocate of the use of anti-psychotic drugs in schizophrenia. But in the summer 1998 edition of *Community Mental Health,* he admitted that these drugs work principally by sedating the patient:

> Sedation, rather than any genuine anti-psychotic effect, is often the main role of standard anti-psychotics.

In 1998, Schizophrenia Ireland, the national schizophrenia association, produced a leaflet which was widely distributed. The leaflet states that this support group 'seeks to provide accurate, factual information about schizophrenia'. But since the medical profession has little accurate, factual information about the nature of schizophrenia, in reality the leaflet reflects current medical opinion. The leaflet emphatically states that 'schizophrenia is *not* caused by pressures within the family'. No evidence exists to prove this. Psychiatry is not even close to establishing what causes schizophrenia. Yet most psychiatrists presume that whatever may be causing this condition, it is not pressures within the family.

No brain malfunction or genetic cause has been demonstrated in schizophrenia. Prematurely, in my view, psychiatrists and GPs concluded that schizophrenia is caused by some as-yet-undiscovered brain abnormality. Doctors treat people on the presumption that they are right with potent drugs which can have horrific side effects. Doctors have long since concluded that it is not worth researching other possible causes of schizophrenia, such as family disharmony, relationship conflicts and social issues. My experience in dealing with people who have been labelled as schizophrenic is that family pressures and disharmony can sometimes play a part in causing schizophrenia.

In recent years, much has been made of the effectiveness and safety of newer drugs for schizophrenia. Such conclusions may be premature. A major study published in the *British Medical Journal* in 2000 analysed fifty-two trials of schizophrenia drugs. The researchers found no difference in effectiveness between older and newer medications.

In a research paper published in the *Ethical Human Sciences and Services Journal* in summer 1999, Al Siebert PhD concluded that the brain disease hypothesis for schizophrenia is actually refuted by all the evidence. He points out that most people with schizophrenia do not progressively deteriorate. They tend to improve over time, which would not occur if a brain chemical abnormality was present:

> Psychotherapy, without medications, has led even the most severely disturbed individuals with schizophrenia to full recovery and beyond.

Many of the features which people commonly believe to be due to chronic mental illness are in fact caused by the treatment these people receive from the medical profession. Take tardive dyskinesia for example. This devastating complication of psychiatric drug treatment causes repetitive involuntary movements which are slow and writhing in a snake-like fashion. The face is most commonly involved, with repetitive sucking or chewing movements, lip movements, tongue movements in and out of the mouth, grimacing and other facial movements. Fidgeting hands, tapping feet and other bizarre involuntary body movements may also occur.

This condition can be extremely distressing to the sufferer, who knows these movements are occurring but cannot stop them. For the person who develops tardive dyskinesia, there is no escape, no respite. Any person who is prescribed a major tranquillizer for more than four to six months may end up with this dreadful condition. Typically once these drugs are prescribed for a schizophrenic patient they are prescribed for many years, often for life.

Using figures made available from psychiatry and the drug industry, Dr Peter Breggin estimated that by 1980 between fifteen and thirty million people worldwide had developed tardive dyskinesia as a result of their medication. It is reasonable to assume that there are a great many more cases now than in 1980, because millions more have been put on these drugs during the intervening years. Research suggests that the risk of developing tardive dyskinesia is 5 per cent after one year of treatment, rising to over 40 per cent after five years. Patients prescribed these drugs are not informed that they are at risk of developing a serious, irreversible, drug-induced neurological disorder.

These figures clearly represent a worldwide epidemic of a devastating and irreversible health problem. The medical profession is usually quick to inform the public at length and in great detail about health problems that reach epidemic proportions. Perhaps psychiatry's reluctance to publicise the tardive dyskinesia epidemic is because psychiatry itself created it.

Psychiatrists are quick to point out that side effects such as tardive dyskinesia occur mainly with the older group of drugs, that this problem is much less likely with newer medications. I am not convinced. This tendency to underestimate the side-effect potential of new drugs is a well established pattern in medicine. A recent legal case in America should serve as a warning for doctors and the public alike. In May 2000, a Philadelphia court awarded 6.7 million dollars to a patient who had developed tardive dyskinesia caused by Risperdal, a new anti-psychotic drug. Could this be just the tip of the iceberg?

Thioridazine (trade name Melleril, Melzine, Thiozine) is a major tranquillizer which has been widely prescribed internationally for well over thirty years. Recently, this drug was associated with a rare but potentially serious type of heart complication. In January 2001, doctors throughout Ireland were notified that the prescribing of thioridazine was to be restricted to schizophrenia only, and only then as a second-line treatment under the supervision of a consultant psychiatrist. In future, patients for whom this drug is prescribed are required to have regular heart checks and blood tests. Why did it take over thirty years to discover this serious side-effect? Since coming on the market, thioridazine has been widely used in the treatment of schizophrenia, agitation, and anxiety. How many people suffered this serious side-effect over the years? How many people may have died as a result?

Dutch psychiatrist Jan Foudraine gradually moved away from the idea that the psychotic person was suffering from a 'disease'. In his book *Not Made Of Wood* he outlines the tendency amongst psychiatrists to believe that their theories are proven facts, and to treat people on this basis:

> I discovered that this idea – that psychotic people are suffering from a 'disease' – was a delusion entertained by a lot of psychiatrists, and very much harder to tackle than the 'fantasies' of people I met in the psychiatric institutions.

Admission to a safe haven has its place. Sometimes people feel so overwhelmed that they need a temporary retreat from the world. Such safe havens were created in the eighteenth century by Phillipe Pinel and other practitioners of 'moral treatment'. Moral treatment involved treating patients with respect and dignity, without cruelty or humiliation. Work and social relationships were encouraged and fostered. Practitioners of moral treatment endeavoured to understand the patient as an individual human being.

Admission to a psychiatric hospital does not necessarily provide a safe haven. Many patients describe admission to a psychiatric hospital as the most terrifying experience of their lives. Psychiatric in-patient treatment is often cold and impersonal. The 'illness' is treated – principally with drugs. The human being is often of secondary importance.

In recent years there have been a few centres in America which provide a safe haven based on principles akin to moral treatment. Soteria House in California was one such centre, run by psychiatrist Loren Mosher. According to Dr Peter Breggin in *Toxic Psychiatry* Soteria House yielded impressive results:

> A series of carefully controlled studies demonstrate the superiority of Soteria for people undergoing their first schizophrenic break compared to a control group sent to a regular mental hospital. In one series only 8 per cent of patients received drugs during their initial stay at Soteria, while *all* of the hospital patients were medicated with the dangerous neuroleptics [major tranquillizers]. In a two-year follow-up, the experimental subjects significantly less often received medications, used less outpatient care, showed significantly better

occupational levels, and were more able to live independently.

In another group of Soteria patients, *none* was given any neuroleptic drugs during the first six weeks and only 10 per cent eventually received them. Again they did better than the matched controls, all of whom were drugged in the regular psychiatric system.

Soteria House was a success story run at a fraction of the cost of a psychiatric unit. The 'recovery-without-drugs' philosophy ran contrary to the prevailing psychiatric reliance on medication. Mainstream psychiatry did not want to know about this method of helping people in emotional turmoil. Funding Soteria House became a problem. The California Department of Mental Health refused to finance it. As Dr Breggin says:

Again we find that the psychiatric monopoly and the psycho-pharmaceutical complex must be broken before significant progress can be made in developing humane, caring, non-medical alternatives. We have a blueprint for easy-to-develop, effective programmes, if only they could get funded.

Cross-cultural studies carried out by the World Health Organisation have found that the outcome for people diagnosed as having schizophrenia is often better in developing countries than in the developed western world. Developing countries were found to have greater social support for patients and to put less emphasis on psychiatric treatment.

Major tranquillizer drugs can sometimes be helpful in a crisis situation. By sedating the person, they may give them some breathing space, a break from the intense emotional experience they are going through. They may calm a person to the point where carers may then be able to get through to them. However, if these major tranquillizers continue to be prescribed for months or years after the crisis, as well as exposing people to their side effects, the resulting sedation may reduce the person's ability to work through the issues relating to their crisis.

MANIC DEPRESSION

When considering the causes of manic depression, the prevailing medical view again favours physical causes such as a brain biochemical imbalance or a genetic defect, despite the fact that no biochemical or genetic abnormality in manic depression has been identified. Doctors base this judgement on the premise that there could not be any other explanation for the major swings of mood experienced by people who have been diagnosed as having manic depression. The mood swings range from deep depression to elation. They could not possibly be caused by emotional or psychological issues. Yet research suggests that the onset of manic symptoms is preceded by stressful life events in more than two-thirds of cases.

This stance fails to take into account that there is at least one condition where people experience extremes of behaviour caused by underlying emotional distress. People who suffer from eating disorders often swing between an abhorrence of food so strong they eat little or nothing (anorexia), and protracted periods of food bingeing where they consume huge amounts of food (bulimia). In my opinion, emotional, psychological and relationship issues are the underlying cause of eating disorders. Sufferers always have desperately low self-esteem.

Just as the swings between anorexia and bulimia relate to underlying emotional issues, the theory that the mood swings in manic depression may originate from emotional and psychological issues is a plausible one. But the medical profession does not seem interested in this possibility. This theory does not fit into the medical view of how things should be, so it is discarded without proper evaluation.

Mania is like a polar opposite to depression. Mania is an escape from enormous inner pain and depression into a fantasy world of elation. But beneath the elation and mania, there often lies a deep sense of worthlessness, hurt and humiliation.

Fred had been diagnosed as having manic depression years before our first meeting. In the early years of our doctor–patient relationship, he could be quite difficult to handle. In subsequent years, we developed a deep trust and mutual respect. Fred's difficult, nit-picking persona masked a deeply vulnerable man. His bouts of mania and depression had more to do with deep-seated emotional distress than a 'mental illness'. A brief history of Fred's life story, told by his son, demonstrates how loneliness, emotional, psychological and relationship conflicts were key issues in Fred's manic depression:

As a small child, I remember very vividly his bad moods and the silences that seemed to go on for days. It seemed as if our house was always filled with tension and I felt relieved when my father was away from home. It was as if I had two fathers. One of them was a kind, caring, loving father; the other man scared me when he woke me at night, shouting at my mother. He sulked over the most trivial things, and many aspects of our family life revolved around keeping him in 'good humour' at all costs.

He was a strict disciplinarian and ruled our home with an iron hand. We all knew who was the boss in no uncertain terms! He made the decisions; no one else was consulted. It was as if he had an enormous need within himself to be in command. No one in my family dared to question him or go against his wishes. He could not handle any threats to his authority. He was *always* right! It makes sense to me now that his chosen career was one where he was very much 'in charge'. In my adult life I can recall a few episodes when I questioned his authority. Although he always apologised to me afterwards, his response each time illustrates his determination to be the 'boss'.

Once he barred me from the family home, putting a chain on the door. Another time he struck me, and on two occasions he demanded immediate payment of a long-term loan he had previously given me. With the possibility of such a response, I didn't have the courage to challenge him too often! He was admitted to hospital on several occasions to be treated for depression. For the last twenty years of his life, he was always on antidepressant medication in one form or another. While he did not like taking any medication, he particularly resented taking lithium. He believed that this drug masked his real self in some way. As for us, as a family, we wanted him to take it because anything that would keep him calm and subdued was better than enduring his mood swings.

Looking back now, I feel both angry and sad that the doctors who treated my father simply plied him with medication and never tried to understand why he was depressed. If the underlying cause of his depression had been explored with him, perhaps he could have emerged from its dark shadows. I recall on one occasion how he was discharged from the psychiatric hospital extremely 'doped' due to a combination of sedatives and antidepressants. He literally did not know what day of the week it was. Alarmed, I phoned his doctor, who told me that my father was now senile and I would have to accept this. I assumed the doctor was right, that he knew what he was talking about. However, my father lived for five years after that incident and he never became senile, up to the day he died. His confusion was entirely due to the drugs prescribed by the 'expert' doctor.

My father's family background was not a happy one. His parents did not communicate very well and his father sought consolation in alcohol. At night, his mother and father sat in separate rooms. His mother entertained visitors in one room while his father was ignored and left sitting in another room. In a similar fashion, in his later years my father often confined himself to one room in the house, cut off from family life for hours on end with only television for company. His mother was obsessed with religion and spent most of her day praying in the church. She was rarely at home, so a housekeeper assumed the mother's role. As he was considered to be a 'difficult child', my father was sent to school at a very young age. Being a small child, he may well have felt this as a form of rejection.

My father liked to travel and went to many exotic places, always on his own. While he was away he was the life and soul of the tour group. He was the centre of attention, and everyone thought he was great fun. We dreaded his return, as he invariably came back from these trips as high as the proverbial kite and had to readjust to mundane home life. I can see now that he had a great need within himself to be liked and accepted. These foreign holidays fulfilled this need, for a while at least. Sometimes he would wear flamboyant clothes.

These made him stand out from the crowd, which was what he wanted, but they were a great source of embarrassment to me. He would often take to the bed for a few days and summon us by means of a bell to wait on him. This was another strategy to get attention.

When he was depressed, he often said that he felt worthless and a burden to my mother and the family. He would often be full of remorse for his behaviour. At times he would dress in a shabby and unkempt manner, giving a visual message to the world as to how he felt about himself. My father was an unhappy man. He provided well for his wife and family, often having to make a little go a very long way. He tried to be the best father he could, given his own family background and the life experiences he had. Though he caused unhappiness to me, I realise now that he never set out to be a bad parent and I bear him no ill will. My relationship with him has healed. My one regret is that during his lifetime, he never had the opportunity to heal himself.

In her book *An Unquiet Mind*, psychiatrist Kay Redfield Jamison writes of her own experience of manic depression. While lithium kept her on an even keel, reducing the extremes of depression and mania, she believes that psychotherapy heals. According to the *Monthly Index of Medical Specialties* – or *MIMS* for short, the reference book doctors refer to when they prescribe medication – lithium's mechanism of action is not known. As in Fred's case, the vast majority of manic depression sufferers receive drug treatment only. Psychotherapy is rarely offered, either as an alternative treatment or in conjunction with medication.

Reflecting on the people I have known who were diagnosed as having manic depression, I noticed that manic episodes typically followed a stressful period or event in their lives. Yet these people were not offered counselling or any other help for the stress in their lives. Many psychiatrists dismiss the value of psychotherapy and counselling in the treatment of manic depression and in the treatment of 'mental illness' in general. A woman from another part of Ireland recently contacted me about her husband who had been treated for manic depression for ten years by the local psychiatrist. She felt that her husband was getting nowhere, and that it might help him to talk to someone about his life and stresses. I agreed, and suggested that she seek out a good therapist in their area. However, when she mentioned to her psychiatrist that they wanted counselling for her husband, the psychiatrist would not hear of it. He was totally against this idea, and threatened to refuse to see him again if he went for counselling.

People diagnosed by the medical profession as having manic depression share the following: very low self-esteem; deep loneliness; major unhappiness and despair in their lives. Before they rush into diagnosing human beings as being 'mentally ill', doctors should explore whether the person's problem can be explained in human terms, in the context of how their life has unfolded for them. By jumping to the 'mental illness' explanation, I believe the medical profession are doing the public a great disservice. In my experience, if you build a trusting relationship with people, giving them time to let them tell you how their life has been for them, there is rarely a need to resort to 'mental illness' explanations.

ANOREXIA AND BULIMIA

In his book *Making the Prozac Decision*, psychiatrist Eliot Kaplan speaks of psychiatry's view of the role of Prozac in the treatment of anorexia:

> What Prozac and other antidepressants can do is to address the underlying biological problem that may be causing the eating disorder.

People reading this are likely to conclude that the cause of anorexia is some 'underlying biological problem'. The truth is that no underlying biological problem as a cause of anorexia has been established. What is presented here as scientific thinking turns out to be little more than wishful thinking.

The *Sunday Independent* carried an article about eating disorders on 12 March 1998. Reporting on the Edinburgh International Science Festival in 1998, journalist Sarah Caden referred to Dr Chris Freeman, a prominent re-searcher who presented a paper at that conference:

> Comparing anorexia to schizophrenia, Dr Freeman recalled that only fifteen years ago, schizophrenia was thought to be caused by the

behaviour of a patient's family. It is now proven,
however, that schizophrenia is genetically
inherited. In another fifteen years, he predicted,
it will be proven that anorexia is also the result
of genetic disorder.

Because there were several inaccuracies in this article, I
wrote to the newspaper to set the record straight. My
letter was published in the *Sunday Independent* the
following week, 19 April 1998:

I cannot allow this statement to go un-
challenged. It is most certainly *not* proven that
schizophrenia is a genetic disorder. The way this
paragraph is structured conveys the clear
impression to the reader that the medical
profession now know for certain that the cause
of schizophrenia is genetic. The truth is that the
medical profession has not yet established the
cause of schizophrenia.

Medical doctors and researchers frequently convey to us
the impression that medical science is making great
strides in its fight against illness. This message comes
across clearly in this article. Referring to Dr Freeman's
comments, the journalist wrote:

Comparing anorexia to schizophrenia, Dr
Freeman recalled that only fifteen years ago,
schizophrenia was thought to be caused by the
behaviour of the patient's family.

In my opinion, this sentence could be interpreted as follows:

> Fifteen years ago, as far as understanding schizophrenia is concerned, we were in the dark ages. We hadn't a clue. Now, though, we really do understand schizophrenia. Now, thanks to medical research, we really do know what it is all about. We have made huge progress in the past fifteen years.

The reality is that modern medicine's understanding of schizophrenia has not changed significantly during the past fifteen years. There have been no major break-throughs, no wonderful discoveries. Dr Freeman, as quoted in the paper, is painting a picture which bears little relation to the truth. I accept that he is being sincere, but in my opinion he is unwittingly misinforming the public. Psychiatry certainly has moved away from the possibility that schizophrenia may be caused by, as Dr Freeman puts it, 'the behaviour of a patient's family'. With no proof to substantiate their stance, psychiatry has formed a strong consensus view that the cause of virtually all so-called 'psychiatric illness' is physical – either genetic, or biochemical, or a mixture of the two.

Referring in my letter to Dr Freeman's predictions about anorexia, I wrote:

> I am fascinated by the sentence 'In another fifteen years, Dr Freeman predicted, it will be proven that anorexia is also the result of a genetic disorder'. As I have not yet perfected the art of reading the future I am personally very

wary of making such a dramatic prediction. I doubt that many psychologists would agree that the cause of anorexia is genetic. At this point in time there is no convincing evidence that anorexia is a genetic illness. Whether there will be in the future remains to be seen.

That Dr Freeman's paper was presented at a scientific meeting did little to allay my concern.

Most of the medical experts who speak so eloquently about anorexia have never suffered from the condition. They have never experienced what a person with anorexia goes through. When those who know most about anorexia – those who have it – describe their experience of this condition, it becomes obvious that severe emotional distress is a key aspect of this eating disorder.

Claire Beeken had anorexia nervosa for thirteen years. Following her recovery, she set up the charity 'Caraline' in England. She named the charity after a friend and fellow sufferer who did not survive the condition. Claire wrote a book describing her life and her anorexia – *My Body, My Enemy: My Thirteen-Year Battle with Anorexia Nervosa.* It becomes quite clear from reading this book that Claire's anorexia had little to do with either a biochemical abnormality or a genetic disorder. Claire's loneliness and emotional suffering scream out at the reader throughout the book.

By the time she wrote the book, she had recovered and had been working for a number of years with her own self-help group. Her words are based on a great deal of personal experience, and the experiences of other people with eating disorders:

There is a common misconception that anorexia is just a diet which got out of hand. But an eating disorder is not a slimmer's disease; rather it is a symptom of stress or other profound emotional damage or psychological problems. About one third of sufferers have been sexually abused; others may have been physically or mentally abused.

Eating disorders can stem from the fracture of a family through divorce or death, the break-up of a relationship, conflict over sexuality, bullying or pressure to achieve.

Throughout her book, Claire Beeken eloquently outlines her own emotional and psychological issues, issues which feature again and again in the lives of people with eating disorders. She describes how in her case the underlying trigger for her eating disorder was sexual abuse, by her grandfather. Her desperately low self-esteem, deep self-rejection and self-hatred are evident throughout her story, as is her intense loneliness and isolation. She speaks of not belonging anywhere, of wanting to disappear, of preferring animals to people because animals 'don't hurt you'.

Claire never opened up to her doctors. She did not trust them or feel safe with them. She spent all her time concealing her problems from the psychiatrists and most of the other healthcare workers. Faced with the prospect of yet another admission to the psychiatric ward:

> I'm terrified of being sectioned [admitted
> against her will]. My life will be in enemy hands
> – even my family won't have a say in what
> happens to me. I'll be forced into hospital
> against my will, forced to stay for six months,
> forced to have treatment, force-fed to be fat.

Claire identifies what in my opinion is the real reason why preoccupation with food becomes such a life-dominating issue for people with eating disorders. Speaking about a friend who later died from anorexia, she writes:

> At sixteen, she started to control her eating – it
> was the only thing in her life that she could
> control.

She describes how, on the rare occasions she felt safe and loved, her eating disorder did not surface:

> I eat well during those three weeks. I feel happy
> and comfortable and the food is lovely. Often
> he [a friend's father] gets us a Chinese takeaway
> and he always has bowls of sweets and fun-size
> chocolate bars dotted around the house. Kim
> stuffs herself – Kim is skinny; and somehow it
> seems okay if I do the same.

Psychiatrists frequently hold case conferences about patients, particularly those who are not responding to treatment. Claire's description of her case conference demonstrates how intimidating and degrading the experience can be for the hapless patient, and how far out of touch psychiatrists can be with their patients:

'Come in,' says Dr Pinto [her psychiatrist] as I tap on the door. I am expecting to see just Dr Pinto, but I open the door and at least half a dozen pairs of eyes swivel in my direction. In the middle of the seated circle sits Dr Pinto. 'Hello, Claire. Come and sit down,' he says, gesturing to the empty chair next to him. This, apparently, is a case conference. 'How do you feel?' 'Do you feel in control when you don't eat?' 'Do you this?' 'Do you that?' There are no introductions, no niceties – these doctors, psychiatrists, nurses, social workers, or whatever they are, launch in with questions from every angle. As I struggle to find an answer to one question, a different mouth chimes in with another query. They are relentless and I am reduced to tears. I feel like a slimy little specimen under a microscope. I pray hard that night. 'Dear Lord Jesus Christ, please let this whole thing be just a nightmare. Please let me wake up at home'. Trouble is, it's very, very real.

The immense intimidation felt by patients during case conferences is echoed in *Out of Me, The Story of a Post-Natal Breakdown* by Fiona Shaw:

The nursing staff seemed as intimidated by the prospect as the patients. I felt on trial there: at first I used to assume that I'd been found guilty and I took what I saw as my punishment quietly. I had Dr A. [her psychiatrist] acting judge. She always seemed to me less interested in finding out what I thought or felt than in having confirmed some assessment she had already made. And in that environment, organised around her own style of communications, all her statements were self-confirming.

When approached holistically the symptoms people present with can, by their symbolism, reveal what the person's real need is. Writing about an episode of binge eating, Claire recognises that she is really trying to satisfy a hunger, not for food, but for love and understanding.

The psychiatrists and their methods played little or no part in Claire's recovery. The first steps on her recovery began when she joined a self-help group for people with eating disorders. Soon after Claire met Lorna, the person running the self-group, a breakthrough occurred:

'Claire,' says Lorna gently, 'all I can see is bone. And look at your pelvic bones,' she says, touching them, 'they're going to come through your skin soon.' 'But I feel so awful,' I wail, wringing my hands. 'I know,' says Lorna softly, giving me a hug. 'I know.' She holds me until I can't cry any more; and a bond begins to form between us.

Psychiatrists believe that people with anorexia deliberately resist the doctor's efforts to help them recover. Indeed, throughout Claire Beeken's book there are many examples of how Claire resisted and thwarted the psychiatrists. This happened, not because Claire wanted to thwart her own recovery, but because she felt so threatened by the psychiatrists and so misunderstood that she felt she had no choice but to resist. Her survival depended on it. In contrast, when confronted by Lorna – someone who understood Claire – she welcomed being challenged:

> Lorna never gives up. When everyone else is letting me away with blue murder, she challenges me. 'I know you're cheating the scales, Claire,' she'll say, matter-of-factly. 'The only person you're hurting is yourself.' And when I retort 'I don't care!' she replies, 'Well, I do.' She works and works at building up my self-esteem, trying to focus on what she perceives as my good points, where I can't see any.

Shortly before she died from anorexia, Claire's friend Caraline spoke to Claire. Caraline had also been through the medical and psychiatric mill, and was none too impressed:

> 'There aren't enough Lornas around, and people need to know that this isn't about slimming, that it goes much deeper than that,' she tells me, adding, 'Doctors need to learn from people like you – someone who knows what it feels like

and who understands. They need to know that brutal treatment doesn't work. The professionals never listened to me; perhaps they'll listen to you.'

Like Claire Beekin, Rosemary Shelly has recovered from anorexia. Editor of the book *Anorexics on Anorexia,* she alludes to patients' lack of emotional support from the medical profession and to doctors' preoccupation with patients' food intake:

Too many hospitalised sufferers are being treated in ways that have proved to be detrimental to their long-term physical and mental health. This is particularly the case when anorexics are fed vast amounts of food to produce rapid weight gain that they are unable to cope with mentally and subsequently lose on discharge from hospital. The patient's mental condition is often overlooked. That should not be the case.

Up to 10 per cent of anorexia sufferers die, either from starvation or suicide. In the six years since Claire Beekin's organisation was founded, none of their clients has died. Is there a message here for the medical profession?

Shelly outlines one anorexia sufferer's experience with the medical profession:

What really surprised and shocked me was the fact that the focus was on feeding me up to produce a change in my body, but never once did they take my mind into consideration. The way I was feeling did not seem important to them. I received very little in the way of counselling.

Eating disorders represent a major challenge to the medical profession. Anorexia does not fit comfortably into traditional medical-disease models. Medical training concentrates on understanding the human body. Understanding human feelings and the psyche barely feature in the training of doctors. Consequently, doctors find themselves out of their depth when faced with people whose deep emotional turmoil is presented in a complex manner, as occurs in anorexia. Not understanding the condition, doctors are often suspicious of eating disorder sufferers. The bemusement and suspicion exhibited by doctors towards eating disorders is, I believe, exemplified in an article in the *Irish Medical News* of 2 November 1998 by Dr Andrew Rynne. An experienced Irish GP and medical journalist, Dr Rynne is rightly seen a modern-thinking and compassionate GP amongst his peers. Dr Rynne was expressing his views while reviewing *Hope – Understanding Eating Disorders*, views which in my opinion make it very difficult to create the open, trusting relationship which is critically important for recovery:

At the very least, anorexia and its accompanying conduct do not fit comfortably into any traditional disease models as I understand them. The cure for all this suffering is in the hands, or at least tantalisingly close to being in the hands, of the sufferers themselves. If the cases described in this book are typical, then so-called eating disorders, anorexia, bulimia and so on, have to be the single most self-centred and self-obsessed type of behaviour on this planet. These people are suffering all right, but they are control freaks. At one level they are 'patients' yet at another level they are power freaks and self-indulgent manipulators and, as such, are extremely powerful attention-seekers.

If, as Dr Rynne says, a condition does not fit comfortably into traditional medical disease models, is it not possible that the problem lies with the disease models rather than the patient? In *Anorexics on Anorexia*, editor Rosemary Shelley outlines the experiences of many contributors to the book as they sought help from their GP for their anorexia:

> Contributors speak of being sent away by their GPs, after initially presenting them with their food problems, and being told to 'Go home and eat' or 'Go for a walk around the garden'. If only it were that simple. To admit to having an eating problem, having the courage to seek medical help, but then being sent away with nothing is humiliating and even fatal.

In my professional experience of people with eating disorders, emotional issues are always the core of the problem. Seventeen-year-old Angela was brought to me by her distraught mother. Angela had been bulimic – repeat-edly inducing herself to vomit her food – for the previous three months. It quickly emerged that Angela had very low self-esteem. She described her relationship with her father as 'difficult'. Angela felt under great pressure to perform well in school examinations.

During that first consultation I explored various aspects of their family relationships with Angela and her mother. I arranged to see Angela and both parents the following day. In a nonjudgemental fashion, I attempted to improve the communication within the family. Angela needed to know she was loved and valued. She was, but she did not realise it. I encouraged both parents to explicitly express their love for Angela to her. Her father explained to Angela that his preoccupation with her exam results stemmed from his love for her. He desperately wanted her to have a much easier life than his. Angela's father's excessive interest in her school performance was, for him, the way he expressed his love for her.

By the end of the second consultation, Angela's whole demeanour had changed dramatically. Initially withdrawn, she was now radiant. During our consultations, one thing became clear to Angela. Her parents loved her dearly, though they had been expressing their love in roundabout, indirect ways. Three months later I met Angela's mother. Angela's bulimic behaviour had not returned. Relationships within the family had improved significantly.

The fact that Angela's problem came to light at an early stage helped to bring the situation to a satisfactory ending.

A GP colleague to whom I recounted this case history

was intrigued by my approach to Angela's bulimia. Recognising his own limited understanding of emotional distress and family relationships – reflecting the medical profession's limited understanding – he replied uncomfortably: 'And I probably would have just put her on Prozac.'

ALCOHOL AND DRUG ABUSE

Drug abuse and alcohol abuse account for most of the remaining 15 per cent of suicides. I do not believe that these are 'psychiatric conditions'. They are caused by a combination of factors: low self-esteem; troubled family relationships; feeling alone and unsafe; lacking emotional closeness to others; social isolation and social problems; painful losses; deep insecurity. These are the central issues behind drug and alcohol abuse. For many people, alcohol is a powerful anaesthetic, temporarily numbing their emotional distress.

Retired professional footballer Paul McGrath enjoyed an illustrious career with Manchester United, Aston Villa and other English clubs. Widely accepted as one of the greatest footballers Ireland has ever produced, Paul is one of Ireland's best loved sportsmen of all time. It is well known that Paul had a 'drink problem'. Paul has spoken openly about this. Indeed, had he not been such a likeable person and such an exceptionally talented player, Paul's excessive drinking would probably have ended his career prematurely. Several managers (including Jack Charlton, the Republic of Ireland manager) forgave him his drinking bouts because he was such a rare talent.

According to psychiatry's logic, Paul McGrath's alcohol problem is a 'psychiatric illness'. But in an Irish television documentary on him broadcast in December 1998 entitled *They Call Him God* Paul eloquently outlined the reason for his excessive drinking. He drank to overcome his extreme shyness. He found it very difficult to talk to people and still does. In the documentary, his wife said that Paul got a sense of self-confidence through her. He had none when he first met her, though he was already a world-class footballer. She spoke of how he had never really been happy before meeting her. Paul had been brought up in an orphanage. He had never known a loving home life as a child.

As I believe is virtually always the case, Paul McGrath's excessive drinking had nothing to do with any 'psychiatric illness'. He drank for human reasons. Paul had low self-esteem; he felt uncomfortable around people. He did not have safe and predictable relationships during his childhood to give him belief in himself and a sense of his own worth. Alcohol helped him overcome his difficulty in communicating with people. It gave him Dutch courage.

In my experience with people who drink excessively, a combination of the following are always present: low self-esteem; insecurity; being easily hurt; fear of facing and dealing with problems; shyness, relationship difficulties; a lack of a sense of safety, predictability and openness within the family when growing up; financial pressures; feeling easily threatened; work stress; inability to say 'no'; great difficulty expressing feelings and emotional needs; bottling up feelings and fears; anxiety; hopelessness; being easily stressed; past experience of many painful losses.

A study carried out in 1998 by doctors at the National Drug Treatment Centre in Dublin revealed that 44 per cent of drug addicts had suffered either physical or sexual abuse when they were young. Some 21 per cent of addicts had been the victims of sexual abuse and a further 23 per cent had been subjected to physical abuse. The researchers found that addicts who had been sexually or physically abused began their drug-taking at an earlier age and found it more difficult to get off drugs. According to the study's co-author Dr Roy Browne, psychiatrist at Cork University Hospital, the link with sexual and physical abuse is a very relevant finding. He said that if the underlying psychological causes of drug abuse are not addressed, many people will be drawn back to heroin. But in my experience, the underlying psychological causes are rarely addressed. This study focused on the link between drug usage and physical and sexual abuse. Had the study also included emotional, psychological and social abuse, it is likely that the final figure would have greatly exceeded 44 per cent.

As with alcohol abuse, drug addiction is not a 'psychiatric condition' and should not be labelled as such. The causes are social, emotional, psychological and troubled relationships. People who have drug or alcohol problems have low self-esteem. Little progress will be made unless raising self-esteem is a core part of the treatment. Rather than label these people 'mentally ill' and treat their 'illness', the medical profession should approach drug addiction in the wider context of the person's life, relationships and experiences. I believe that overcoming substance abuse is far more likely when the issues which prompted the abuse are addressed.

5

WHY PEOPLE KILL THEMSELVES – THE MEDICAL VIEW

Most doctors believe that over 70 per cent of suicides are caused by depression, 15 per cent by schizophrenia, and most of the remaining 15 per cent by psychiatric conditions such as alcohol and drug abuse, anorexia and anxiety.

THEORY AS FACT; NON-SCIENCE AS SCIENCE

In medicine as in life in general, when a theory is repeated often enough it can eventually become accepted as fact. This is especially likely when the theory is one which is beneficial to the medical profession, compatible with the profession's beliefs and practices. Doctors look at the problem of suicide through the lens of psychiatric illness. The resulting tunnel vision prevents doctors from taking a broader, more holistic approach to suicide.

Doctors increasingly believe that the most likely fundamental underlying cause of suicide is an imbalance of chemicals in the brain. While many psychiatrists believe that 90 per cent of suicides are due to 'mental illness', this does not mean that they are right. Modern medicine bases this belief on psychological autopsies, which the profession rates highly. But these autopsies are no more than a psychiatric interpretation of the events preceding the suicide. If the psychiatrist is biased the psychological autopsy will also be biased, albeit unconsciously.

Medical experts instinctively look for evidence of psychiatric illness following a suicide rather than seeking to understand the human pain and despair which brought that person to the point where no other option held any attraction for them. As a group, psychiatrists cannot – or will not – seriously consider the possibility that social, emotional, psychological and relationship problems provide sufficient cause for a person to take their own life. The medical explanation of suicide is never complete without reference to the central role of 'psychiatric illness'. I believe this view does not reflect the reasons why people choose to take their own lives.

Certainly, many people who take their lives are depressed. There is a great deal of depression, anguish and despair in our society. What I am questioning is the labelling of this emotional turmoil as 'mental illness'. Emotional distress is understandable and appropriate in the context of how that person's life has unfolded for them. Unfortunately, such an approach is alien to modern psychiatry's preoccupation with mental illness – diagnosing, labelling and prescribing.

Doctors tend to believe so much in their theories that they become convinced of their validity, even when there is little solid evidence to back them up. Once theories compatible with medical philosophy and practice become accepted as fact, there are many benefits for the medical profession:

- Theories are questionable, facts are not. In discussions and arguments either with the general public or groups who question medical practice, theories will always have to be vigorously shown to be better then other possible theories. Not so with facts. Facts have passed through the questioning stage.

- Psychiatrists become society's experts on suicide since they are the experts on 'mental illness' because they are in possession of the 'facts'.

- Those who believe that psychiatry's approach to suicide is seriously misguided can be easily dismissed. Having 'established' that mental illness is the key issue in suicide, psychiatrists can easily ignore dissenters who question their beliefs and practices.

Governments, the media and the public alike take their lead from medical experts. Consequently newspaper articles on depression and suicide fall into this 'presenting theory as fact' trap. We have now reached the point where medical theories on mental illness and suicide have become widely accepted as established fact. Hardly a week goes by without this sort of misinformation appearing in the national media. There is rarely a rush from within the medical profession to correct the misinformation via the 'Letters to the Editor' column the following week. I believe that this may be because the misinformation strengthens the position of the medical profession, conveying the impression that doctors understand more about these issues than they actually do.

Is the Prevailing Medical View Right?

When expert doctors speak about health matters few people feel confident and knowledgeable enough to challenge them publicly. It is not easy for non-medical people to question doctors. The medical profession quickly respond to such challenges with complex language and statistics which confuse even the most tenacious and persistent questioner, putting him in his place. But it is vitally important that the pronouncements of the medical profession are challenged, to test whether they are as valid as they seem.

Journalist John Waters is not impressed by the 'mental illness' theory as the cause of suicide. In *The Irish Times* of 13 January 1998 he wrote:

> One of the traditional cop-outs about suicide has been that it is the consequence of mental illness. The purpose of emphasising this connection has been to spare the families of suicide victims but also society at large from the guilt arising from the accusation that a suicide might otherwise represent. There have been strenuous attempts of late to create a causal link between suicide and what is called depression. Indeed, in a recent interview, psychiatrist Dr Patrick McKeon reiterated the conventional view that the vast majority of

suicide victims have been suffering from 'some underlying psychiatric problem, mainly depression or mood disorders'.

Later in the same interview, Dr McKeon spoke more specifically about the nature of what is called depression. Dr McKeon said that 'human beings, to live with themselves, have a natural infusion of positive perspectives on things, that enables us to keep going in life. When that's taken away, that's actually called depression.' This suggests to me that depression is not simply a clinical condition that descends on the individual like a virus. It is inextricably related to the external conditions of that human being's life and his perceptions of these. To say that suicide victims are depressed is telling us nothing. Everyone gets depressed but not everyone commits suicide.

In my opinion, John Waters makes far more sense on suicide than many psychiatrists. When I read what psychiatrists say about why people end their own lives, I often feel a serious lack of human understanding.

PSYCHOLOGICAL AUTOPSIES: A CRITIQUE

When a person dies and the doctors do not know the cause of death, an autopsy is carried out. During this post-mortem examination the pathologist examines the body, searching for the cause of death. Autopsies have been carried out for decades. They are an established part of modern medicine's efforts to identify the cause of death. Psychological aut-

182

opsies have become popular within modern medicine as a method of identifying why people end their lives. In a psychological autopsy, the events prior to the suicide are examined by doctors for evidence of 'mental illness'.

Psychiatrists try to get as much information as possible about the person's psychological state preceding the suicide. They piece together a psychological picture of the person which might provide some clues as to why that person took their own life. Doctors find enough information to make a post-mortem diagnosis of a 'mental illness' in over 90 per cent of suicides, even if the person has never seen a doctor or psychiatrist.

Psychiatrists approach a psychological autopsy from the perspective of psychiatry. Psychiatrists will speak to family members and friends, looking for clues and signs, not of emotional distress, but of what psychiatrists believe to be psychiatric illnesses. Before they even begin the autopsy, they are heavily prejudiced in favour of making a psychiatric diagnosis.

A psychological autopsy is based on opinions, not facts. A psychological autopsy carried out by a psychologist or psychotherapist might come to a totally different conclusion to the one arrived at by a psychiatrist. What a psychiatrist decides is definite evidence of a 'diagnosable psychiatric disorder' might well be interpreted by an experienced psychologist or psychotherapist as evidence of severe emotional distress. But the psychiatrist's view will override that of the psychologist's because psychiatrists are deemed to be the real experts.

I believe modern medicine's heavy reliance on psychological autopsies is open to question. Major conclusions are being drawn from these autopsies; conclusions which are being accepted as facts, upon which future health policies on suicide are based. Psychiatrists regularly quote psychological autopsies as proof that 'psychiatric illness' is the chief cause of suicide. But this is only one of several possible interpretations. The following tragic case demonstrates how inaccurate psychological autopsies can be.

In his mid-twenties, John took his own life. His distraught family could not understand why in the prime of his life he had ended it all. John seemed to have everything going for him. He had just completed a university degree course in Dublin. John started his first job three weeks before his suicide.

Kathy, John's sister, attended me two months after his death. Prior to meeting Kathy, I had not met John or any of the family. Kathy came to me because she was suffering the intense pain of losing a loved one through suicide. She was deeply confused and hurt. She could not understand why John had not come to her or the family for help. Why had he killed himself now, when things were really falling into place for him? John had his degree, his job, his independence, money. Why suicide? Why now? It just didn't make sense. John did not leave a suicide note to explain his reasons.

The pain and loss experienced by people bereaved by suicide is so intense that words cannot describe it. The grieving process following the death of someone close to our hearts is always painful and prolonged. When the death occurs because the person has decided to end their own life, the grief and loss become even more unbearable. Kathy attended me for six months. She gave me a comprehensive history of the family life which she and John had experienced. She also presented me with a detailed picture of John's external world, his life as she saw it. I tried to feed back to her how John may have felt at various times in his life – to show her his internal world, that crucially important part of each of us which we rarely feel safe enough to discuss with others. When our sessions concluded, we both felt we understood – to some degree, at least – why John had ended his life.

To the outside world, John's life might have seemed quite normal and ordinary. John was the youngest of four children. Kathy was second-youngest in the family, two years older than John. John and Kathy had always been close. The family had lived in Dublin. Kathy moved to Limerick six months before John's death.

Kathy recalled that their father was an aggressive, unpredictable man. Their mother was very quiet. Every day their father would become aggressive at home. Their mother, being very passive, did not intervene. She was scared to stand up either for herself or for the children. Communication between their parents deteriorated steadily through the years of marriage. As a result, the younger children (Kathy and especially John), bore the brunt of their father's frustration and aggression. By the time he first went to school, John was already shy and timid. His experience at school heightened John's sense of fear and isolation. For years he screamed and did everything possible to avoid going to school.

Kathy said that neither parent acted on John's pleas regarding school – quite the opposite. John was physically punished by his father for trying to avoid going to school.

John's mother did not have the courage either to tackle the problems at school or to stop her husband from beating John when he kicked up a fuss every morning before school.

Life seemed to improve for John between the ages of ten and thirteen. A talented soccer player, he played with the local football team in Dublin. He was popular, and was getting attention and praise from the team, the coaches and the supporters. Some of his emotional needs were being met. However, this stopped when he entered the teenage years, as he withdrew from sports after a minor row with his team-mates.

John finished school and qualified some years later with a university degree. Kathy recalled that while at university, he had seemed happy. John had a hectic social life and seemed to have plenty of friends. Soon after he received his degree, the time came to take up his first job. The family noticed that during the three months which preceded his suicide, he became increasingly withdrawn. John stayed at home virtually all the time, often staying in bed most of the day, not wanting to meet people, even his own family. He appeared very anxious and frightened. The least thing would greatly increase his anxiety. Then John decided to end it all and took his own life.

To understand the potential for misinterpretation when relying on psychological autopsies carried out by modern medicine, here is an account of how a psychological autopsy on John's suicide might be interpreted, followed by what I believe is a far more accurate assessment of why he took his own life. In John's case, psychiatrists would probably conclude that John ended it all because he had a 'psychiatric illness'. They would interpret his staying in bed during the day, his withdrawal, his depressed mood to be sure signs of a severe clinical depression. Psychiatrists would confidently state that he fulfilled the previously mentioned criteria for depression which are widely accepted within psychiatry.

According to the *Diagnostic and Statistical Manual IV*, a psychological autopsy on John's life would find that at least six of the criteria required to diagnose a major depressive episode were present before his death:

Criterion A1: He was depressed, sad, hopeless and discouraged for two to three months prior to his suicide.

Criterion A2: John clearly had lost interest in many things, and there was virtually no pleasure in his life during his final months.

Criterion A3: His appetite was much reduced in the final months. He frequently skipped meals. He had lost interest in food.

Criterion A4: His sleep was disturbed for several weeks before his death. At times he would sleep most of the day as well as night (hypersomnia). At other times, he was very agitated at night, and could not sleep (insomnia).

Criterion A5: At times John was very agitated and restless. At other times he was the opposite, and would gaze absently for hours at the television.

Criterion A6: John's suicide took a considerable

amount of pre-planning, given the means he ended his life (in order to protect confidentiality I will not go into the method he used). John must therefore have had suicidal ideas in the hours, days or possibly weeks before his suicide.

John met these six criteria. Only five criteria need to be met in order to diagnose a 'major depressive episode'. The result of John's psychological autopsy is conclusive: John took his life because he was suffering from a 'Major Depressive Episode'. He is entered as another statistic, further proof that psychiatric illness is the underlying cause of suicide.

I believe that psychological autopsies miss the point, due to the unconscious prejudice of the psychiatrists who carry them out. They should really be called 'psychiatric autopsies' because they are carried out under the supervision of psychiatrists. We do not need labels or psychiatric diagnoses to understand why people kill themselves. They end their lives for human reasons. They feel desperately unsafe in this world. They have lost all hope.

What young children most need in their formative years is unconditional love and acceptance, from their parents but also from the other important people in their life, including extended family and teachers. If children feel loved and accepted unconditionally as they are growing up, they naturally develop high self-esteem, and people with high self-esteem tend not to take their own lives. However, if the growing child does not feel that he is loved and accepted unconditionally in his life, he begins to feel threatened, unsafe. Children have a deep need to create as much safety as possible for themselves in their lives. They (often subconsciously) develop strategies – protectors – to help them cope in a family and in a life which to them does not feel safe.

One of the most common protectors human beings use when feeling threatened is avoidance. If something scares the daylights out of us, our first impulse is to run away. John's tendency to avoid when feeling unsafe began at a very young age, though it went unnoticed within the family. Children have a natural tendency to reach out to their parents for hugs and physical comforting. John's father was an unpredictable man. He was not very good at physically showing any affection to anyone. John soon learned that if he reached out to his father, his father might well ignore him. By the time John was four years of age, he was cautious about reaching out to his father. Painful as it was for John not to reach out to the father he loved, it was better than reaching out and being ignored – better than having his approval-seeking gesture rejected. Rejection is painful at any age. To a small child it is devastating.

Primary school was tough going for John. For many years he cried every morning, begging his parents not to send him to school. John was having great difficulty coping with his teachers. He told his parents this, but they did not act on it. His parents became sick and tired of his behaviour every school morning. They regularly lost their temper with John, lifting him into the car against his will and bringing him to school. John was regularly humiliated, beaten, ridiculed and criticised in school.

John's father was rarely at home. When he was, he was at best unpredictable and often aggressive. Being a passive person, John's mother felt unable to stand up for him. Traumatised and feeling unsafe, John increasingly withdrew into himself, even in his childhood years. John's quietness and shyness was commented on at school. I believe that subconsciously John chose the strategy of avoidance and quietness. If he did not take any risks and kept his mouth shut, there was less chance of him being criticised, ridiculed, rejected, laughed at, humiliated or beaten, either at home or at school.

As a young teenager, he was emotionally vulnerable. John had to protect himself from further hurt, criticism and rejection in any way he could. Sport was one of the few things he felt confident about during his teenage years. John knew he was good at soccer. Through sport he got approval, praise and social contact. But he remained emotionally fragile during these adolescent years. Being so easily hurt and needing to avoid rejection so badly, John suddenly gave up soccer after a minor disagreement with his team-mates and never played again. He lost all the friends he had gained through sport. His withdrawal from people and from life gathered momentum during his teenage years.

John did well enough in his Leaving Certificate exams to go to university. According to friends he made there, he was popular and well liked. His sister told me that his time at university was good for him. But when he finished his final exams, his tendency to avoid resurfaced. He stayed at home all day. John withdrew from his friends. He also withdrew emotionally from his family, even from Kathy to whom he had previously been close. Suicide was his final act of avoidance. John could not take any more pain.

In every case I have encountered, emotional, social, psychological, self-esteem and relationship issues lie at the heart of suicide. I passionately believe that parents do the best they can for their children, in accordance with their own level of self-esteem and their own experience of life. It is inappropriate to blame parents or the family when loved ones take their own lives. As long as the medical profession continues to underestimate the role of self-esteem, relationships, emotional, psychological and social issues, I believe that medical intervention will not reduce the suicide rate. The public, particularly those at risk of suicide, deserve better.

Why People Kill Themselves – Do Doctors Differ?

The prevailing view within modern medicine is that 90 per cent of those who take their lives are 'psychiatrically ill'. For example, a County Mayo psychiatrist wrote in the *Irish Medical News* of 7 September 1998 that suicide occurs almost exclusively in psychiatrically ill patients. Similarly, according to the 1998 Aware publication *Suicide in Ireland: A Global Perspective and A National Strategy*, over 90 per cent of suicides were mentally ill. In an interview published in the *Irish Medical News* of 6 November 2000, Dr Pat McKeon, consultant psychiatrist and medical director at St Patrick's Hospital, Dublin, discussed his views on the causes of suicide. According to the interview, Dr McKeon stated that 'an underlying psychiatric question' is the first key factor in suicide.

However, not all doctors concur with this view. In an interview in *Medicine Weekly* in October 1998, Dr R. F. Chute, the coroner for west Kerry, stated that the majority of young male suicides have no history of psychiatric illness. In the *Sunday Business Post* newspaper in November 1998, Professor Anthony Clare did not mention mental illness as he discussed the possible reasons for the increasing rate of young male suicides:

> Young men are killing themselves at ever-increasing numbers at the present time, and while a variety of explanations have been suggested – unemployment, drugs, alcohol, a lack of self-esteem in contemporary males – the precise explanation or explanations remain mysterious.

In an interview with journalist John Waters in *The Irish Times* of 8 January 1991, Dr Bartley Sheehan, Dublin GP and coroner gave his views on suicide:

> Suicide is a response to the individual's perception of their circumstances and their experience. What suicide means for the individual is that there has been the loss of something essential to that individual maintaining their life. I think it's the loss of a deeply held personal aspiration, some private ambition, some view of the direction of their lives, and which they've recognised the absolute loss of. That is gone and, consequently, their life is no longer worth living.

In the *Irish Medical Times* of 7 June 1996, Dr Sheehan expressed his concerns about modern medicine:

> I believe that the medical establishment is so limited in its perspective and it is dominated by doctors who have very limited experience of the real world.

A 1998 study on attitudes to suicide among thirteen- and fourteen-year-old Irish schoolchildren by Dr M. O'Sullivan and Professor M. Fitzgerald was published in the *Journal for the Association of Professionals in Services for Adolescents*. The researchers found that these teenagers looked on suicide as solving a problem. The acceptance of suicide as a problem-solving exercise among schoolchildren was described as a 'striking feature' by the authors of this study. Dr O'Sullivan and Professor Fitzgerald concluded that society needs to address the social nature of suicide.

Most medical experts do not accept that suicide can be explained by understanding how the person sees himself, his life, his relationships and his experiences. In philosophical terms, this latter approach is known as existentialism. In a lecture to the 1998 national conference of the Association of Hospice and Allied Bereavement Group, Irish psychologist Maurice Ward recommended that:

> Medical experts should add to the volume of statistical and medical information available on suicide by looking at the problem in a more

existential way. People bereaved by suicide are never inside that event. This keeps people from accepting what that person might be going through. When people talk about the statistical end of things – and of course some people are at greater risk – they talk about depression, alcoholism, etc. I'm looking at the psychological processes that a [suicidal] person might be going through.

Maurice Ward added that he hoped his work would shine light on other facets of the suicide problem that often do not receive attention. I am not confident that modern medicine will listen to Maurice Ward's advice. After all, he is only a psychologist, and how could a psychologist know more than a doctor? Psychiatry has not researched the existential theory of suicide in nearly as much detail as the biological theory. The latter is much more in keeping with the values and beliefs of psychiatry. If the existential theory were proven to be the cause of suicide, rather than the biological theory, psychiatrists might find themselves out of a job. I am not surprised that most psychiatrists show little enthusiasm for theories which might diminish the prestige and position of psychiatry.

6

—

WHY PEOPLE KILL THEMSELVES: AN ALTERNATIVE VIEW

WHY DO PEOPLE TAKE THEIR OWN LIVES?
The majority of people who take their own lives

- Have low self-esteem
- Do not feel safe and secure within themselves
- Are emotionally very vulnerable
- Have a major conflict within themselves: conflict between the human need to be accepted by others as they really are and the fear of being rejected, of not being good enough. So they put on a front, an outward show. People are often astounded when people who were 'the life and soul of the party' or people who outwardly 'had everything to live for' take their own life. The greater the distance between the image a person presents to the world – their 'mask' – and their real self, the more lonely and hopeless they feel, and the more likely they are to take their own life, seeing no other way out of their pain.
- Lack intimacy in their lives. They may well have people

in their life who really love them. But many people are terrified of opening up even to the people they love and who love them, terrified of being seen to be vulnerable.

- Lack unconditionally loving supportive relationships with people who will accept them as they are, or are afraid to reveal their true selves even to those who do love and support them unconditionally
- Have been abused either sexually or physically, or have had troubled relationships in their family of origin
- Have experienced hurts and losses which are too painful to endure
- Find themselves ostracised in some way from important people in their life or from society in general
- Find themselves faced with intolerable obstacles to overcome in their lives; obstacles which seem impossible to overcome

A fundamental need of every child is to be loved and accepted unconditionally. The more conditions that a child feels are attached to the love bond between child and parents, the more insecure the child will feel (e.g. I must always be top of the class, I must be on the school football team, I must always be good, I must always be nice, I must not get angry, I must never upset Mummy/ Daddy, I must go to university, I must not fail my exams). In open relationships within the family, children feel they can be open about themselves and know love will not be withdrawn. Such relationships foster high self-esteem in children. In later life, people brought up in such a home environment find it easier to create loving, emotionally intimate relationships with others than people who did not have open loving relationships with their parents.

While modern medicine concentrates almost all its suicide research on establishing that suicide is primarily a 'psychiatric' problem, the human factors which bring people to the point of suicide are calling for attention. Much current suicide research is focusing on 'the suicidal brain'. I would much prefer to see the focus on 'the suicidal mind' or, better still, 'the suicidal person'. These are some of the social, emotional, psychological, relationship and cultural issues which can drive people to take their own lives:

Loneliness

So common is loneliness nowadays that it is akin to an epidemic. Tragically, it is a silent epidemic. In a society which expects us to be successful and upbeat about life, there are few people to whom we can express our loneliness. The degree of loneliness may vary from mild, infrequent loneliness to an ever-present torrent of emotion whose depth words cannot describe. Most people who take their lives have reached a point of unbearable loneliness. The pain which deep loneliness brings can become too much to live with.

The people who are suffering from so-called 'mental illnesses' which doctors say are the underlying cause of suicide – depression, schizophrenia, alcohol and drug abuse and other conditions such as eating disorders and anxiety – have one thing in common. They are often very lonely people. The degree of loneliness a person experiences in their life can often be traced back to their childhood. Sometimes the child feels the loneliness at the time, but often the depth of the pain is so overwhelming that the child suppresses it rather than feel such emotional distress. Suppressed feelings remain with the person. Later in life, the pain may resurface, resulting in anxiety, depression or other forms of emotional distress which doctors label and treat as 'mental illness'.

Families that seem particularly likely to create lonely children are those where one or both parents have a drink problem; where one parent is aggressive and the other is passive and does not confront the aggressor; where parents are unhappy and unfulfilled in their relationship; where children are not given the freedom to express how they feel freely, for fear of upsetting their father or hurting their mother or vice versa. Children of parents who have had a so-called 'psychiatric illness' for many years often experience deep loneliness. Their distressed parent may have become so preoccupied with themselves and their own survival that they are unable to meet the emotional needs of their children or form an emotionally intimate relationship with them. Families where one or both parents are away a lot, or preoccupied with work and other activities are more likely to produce lonely children. So are homes where there is little or no expression of love. Children need to be told over and over again by their parents that they are loved, and they need bagfuls of hugs to prove it. Sometimes there is a major imbalance; one parent may be emotionally remote from the children and may not communicate love to them, while the second parent is at the other extreme, almost smothering the children with love.

People hide their loneliness because it is not publicly acceptable to be lonely. You do not have to be alone to be lonely. I have met many lonely individuals who always have people around them. But it is not enough to be surrounded by people, even family and friends, unless you can be yourself with them. We all wear a mask. We reveal to others only what we feel safe to reveal. The more of ourselves we need to conceal, the more lonely we will be.

Everyone who knows Marie thinks of her as a bubbly, cheerful person. Marie knows different. Behind that mask of humour and frivolity lies much loneliness and sadness. Marie knows that her humour is a front. She recently showed me a piece she wrote, as if talking to this cheerful mask. I was so touched, I asked her if I could include it in this book. She calls her humorous mask 'Coco the Clown':

Hi Coco,
I am so glad you are part of my life. I know the going must be difficult for you at times. You are called upon almost daily. I never realised before now what you mean to me. I feel safe when you're around. Maybe I even overuse you. I certainly hide behind you; some people know only you. I feel really lost and abandoned when you're not around or when people don't quite get your drift. You first came into my life when I was a lonely child. I was so careful to keep you to myself, until I realised that other people enjoyed you. I know I probably depend on you too much, but then again, you are my best

friend. Thank you for all the support and shelter you have provided. I don't know where we go from here, but I hope you will always be a part of my life.

Marie recently noticed that she goes into this humorous mode when she feels threatened in social situations, or in situations likely to evoke great sadness. The greater the likelihood that she will experience despair and loss, the stronger her urge to laugh her way around the situation. This desire to behave in the opposite way to how one is feeling is an understandable human response to overwhelming despair, a way of protecting oneself from fully experiencing sadness and loss.

Loss and Hurt

The loss of what is cherished can be devastating. The pain and emotional hurt is sometimes so great that suicide seems the only way to kill the pain. There are countless examples, depending on the person's life circumstances and experiences – loss of love and intimacy following the ending of a relationship or the death of a loved one; the loss of status and usefulness which occurs when people retire or when the kids fly the nest. The loss of what might have been – the woman who desperately wants children but cannot have them; the man who desperately wanted promotion but was passed over. The loss of one's health can lead to depression and suicide. There is also the loss of hope for the future – losing hope that anyone will ever love them or be there. A person's decision to end their life in reaction to a particular loss or trauma may seem excessive, but the final trigger is usually the straw that broke the camel's back. The person has reached a state of such despondency that it does not take much to send them over the edge. There have been too many losses and broken dreams, too many hurts and rejections, creating a depth of despair where every possible solution looks hopeless. In such a state, like the fighter pulverised by his opponent, the final blow may seem light enough. By then they have thrown in the towel. There is no fight left in them.

Public humiliation with the accompanying loss of face and status can be devastating enough to trigger suicide. Losing face can be very difficult to deal with. The successful businessman who goes bankrupt. The previously successful student who flunks an exam. A dark secret which suddenly surfaces to the cold light of day for all to see and judge. Facing people can be very difficult when you feel that you have let yourself or others down. Losing face is linked to self-esteem. The lower a person's self-esteem, the more painful it is to be seen to fail in public. Sometimes it is less painful to end one's life than to live with the pain of losing face.

Many people believe that suicide is a selfish act, that the suicidal person should cop on to themselves and remember the loss their loved ones will suffer if they take their own lives. In fact, most suicidal people believe they are such a burden that those people around them would be better off without them.

Social Upheaval and Change
Suicide rates are affected by changes in society. Social changes which unite people and communities reduce the

suicide rate. When a country is at war, you might think that more people would be inclined to take their own lives. Actually the suicide rate tends to drop. This is probably because the national sense of unity and pride brings people closer together, creating a powerful community spirit. On the other hand, the suicide rate increases when social changes isolate people, reducing people's sense of hope, identity and belonging.

The dramatic increase in the suicide rate of young men reflects how enormously the lives of men have changed during the past thirty years. Three decades ago, men earned the family income and women stayed at home to look after the family. Both sexes had a sense of who they were and what was expected of them. While the role of women in society has expanded dramatically, the role of men has been eroded. Some men do not know how to cope with this.

Superficially, the young male lives the life of Riley compared to his counterparts of thirty years ago – sex, drugs, freedom, alcohol, drugs, no religious oppression, no corporal punishment at school. But inside, many young men are very unsure of themselves and their role in modern society. From an early age boys are conditioned – at home, at school, among their friends and in the media – not to show their feelings. In the process, young men are given the message that they must hide away a core part of who they are: their feelings, their vulnerability, their fear of not being good enough, of not meeting the expectations they believe others have of them.

Men become increasingly afraid of – and therefore avoid – intimacy, true closeness with others, even loved ones. They play a dangerous game called 'big boys don't cry'. Sometimes men reach a point of utter desperation when the game of life is too painful. For men conditioned not to ask for help, not to show vulnerability, suicide becomes a real option: a way to end their pain without losing face.

Nowadays the role of women has expanded greatly. As well as their historical role as the child-bearer and home-maker, women can take on virtually everything that was traditionally the domain of men. For some young women who feel there is no purpose to their lives, there is one option which young men do not have: they can have a child. Suddenly life has a purpose. The mother is import-ant. She has a child, someone to love, to look after – a child who will love her in return. People who used to ignore her now come over to her and admire the baby. In general, society rallies around her. She may receive some assistance from the State. In contrast, men are becoming less and less essential to the everyday life of society. There are many families where women are now rearing children with little or no input from the father.

A record number of suicide victims were found during 1998 in a forest at the foot of Japan's Mount Fuji. Has there been a massive outbreak of psychiatric illness in Japan, which would explain, in psychiatry's language, why Japan has experienced a dramatic suicide-rate increase? Hardly. However, there *was* a major social crisis in Japan in 1998. Their economy virtually collapsed. Japanese authorities suspect that the increased rate of suicide is linked to the increased fear, uncertainty and hopelessness experienced by Japanese citizens as a consequence of the economic collapse.

Relationship Issues

Research suggests that people are compelled to take their lives by conflict within an important relationship in their lives. Medical research has found that suicide is closely linked to how human beings bond with each other in relationships. For every human being, their first and most powerful experience of bonding occurs in their own home. How people bond with others in their adult life will therefore be influenced by how safe and secure they felt within the key relationships of their childhood.

According to the Samaritans, the reason most cited by those who attempt suicide is that there were relationship difficulties. The enormous changes in a person's life created by the break-up of a relationship or a marital separation can be overwhelming. Add to this the immense guilt and loss which separating or divorcing parents experience regarding their children. The end result can be a tidal wave of emotional pain and social alienation which in the words of one client of mine, 'makes three feet of rope sound attractive'.

Psychological research suggests that when parents break up, boys do not cope as well as girls, and that they suffer much more psychological stress. Usually the mother gets custody of the children. Mothers and daughters become closer to each other and develop a mutually supportive relationship. Boys, however, feel themselves being rigidly controlled by their mothers and find it more difficult to form a mutually supportive relationship with their mothers.

The number of suicide attempts increases around St Valentine's Day and Christmas Day. Dr J. Birtle and his colleagues noticed that an unusually high number of people had taken an overdose of drugs and presented to casualty departments on St Valentine's Day. They carried out a study to evaluate this link in more detail and published their results in the *British Medical Journal* of 24 March 1990. The study involved three health districts in the Birmingham area over five years (1983-8). The researchers concluded that there was an association between St Valentine's Day and suicide attempts, particularly in suicide attempts by adolescents. They also found that there was a link between suicide attempts and Christmas Day.

The researchers concluded that:

> Those in contact with adolescents should be particularly vigilant during emotionally charged festivals such as Christmas Day and St Valentine's Day. Previous studies have shown an association between suicide attempts and stressful events such as an unsuccessful relationship, unemployment, and physical illness. The festival of St Valentine's Day may induce stress due to unrequited love.

There is no evidence that a massive outbreak of 'mental illness' occurs every year on St Valentine's Day and Christmas Day. The triggers for suicide attempts are human issues, not 'psychiatric illness'.

Sexuality

There is substantial evidence that young homosexual men are much more likely to take their lives than heterosexual males. This cannot be put down to psychiatric illness. Homosexuality is not currently viewed as a mental illness, though it is only a few decades since it was viewed as such by the medical profession and by society in general.

Homosexuals encounter many psychosocial problems which their heterosexual counterparts never have to deal with. According to the American Academy of Paediatrics' *Statement on Homosexuality and Adolescence*, October 1993:

> The psychosocial problems of gay and lesbian adolescents are primarily the result of societal stigma, hostility, hatred, and isolation.

In *Gay Community News* in October 1998, journalist Cathal Kelly questioned the continuing silence around suicides among gay youth:

> The figures for gay youth suicide are stark. Twelve different studies in North America between 1972 and 1994 show that an average of one-third of young gay men attempted suicide, with nearly 40 percent of these making repeated attempts. The rate of suicide attempts among young gay men was found to be ten times higher that the attempt rate for young men generally. Two further studies published earlier this year (1998) confirmed that young gay men are seven to thirteen times more likely to commit suicide than heterosexual men.

Issues around sexuality can be deeply threatening for young people. There is a great deal of peer and advertising pressure on young people around sex and sexuality. Struggling to come to terms with sex and relationships, teenagers often find themselves without the support and understanding of the key people in their lives – their parents. Many parents avoid discussing sexual issues with their children. Many teenagers are reluctant to discuss sexual issues with their parents. When parents are open to discussing sexual matters, their children have that option open to them if they wish to avail of it. The issue of sexuality needs to be discussed and explored far more openly in our society.

Hopelessness
Modern medicine accepts that when people feel they have no hope for the future, they are more likely to end their life. Medical experts say that hopelessness occurs as a result of depression. The next step in the medical scheme of things is to treat the depression with antidepressants in order to lift the depressive illness. The theory is that the hopelessness will also improve as a consequence. But hopelessness is not a 'mental illness'. It is a human reaction when life becomes overwhelming. A person becomes hopeless when they see no way out of their crisis; things will never improve. At that moment no option other than suicide seems likely to end their torment. Many people will take their own lives rather than acknowledge their excruciatingly painful emotional vulnerability.

People with serious illnesses sometimes reach the

point of complete hopelessness and decide to end it all. Any serious medical condition where the person experiences constant pain and loss (of mobility, independence, hope) may drive sufferers to the point of suicide. Illnesses that seriously undermine quality of life and are not likely to improve may bring people to the point of despair, where suicide becomes a possible way out of their misery.

Marital Status

Modern medicine has long recognised that marital status has a bearing on an individual's suicide risk. Married people have the lowest suicide rates, followed by single people, widowed, divorced and separated people in that order. Unhappily married men and women are more likely to end their lives than those whose marital relationships are happy and fulfilling. Married people have a partner with whom they share their lives. While many single people are perfectly happy either to be in relationships or not, as suits the individual, others do feel the lack of an intimate relationship in their lives. The three groups of people most likely to take their lives – the widowed, the divorced and the separated – have one thing in common. Their marital relationship has ended, leaving them without their most intimate relationship, which had been so important in their lives.

Research suggests that the rate of suicide following divorce or separation is substantially higher in men than in women. Following divorce or separation, men's access to their children may be considerably restricted. In disputes over custody of the children, the courts tend to favour the mother as the principal custodian. As a result, men may find themselves deprived of close, frequent contact with their children, while the contact which these fathers do have with their children may no longer be within the familiar surroundings of the family home. In the interests of minimizing the children's upheaval, the man is more likely to have to leave the family home than his partner, often having to set up home away from friends and neighbours. Consequently, men may find themselves disconnected from important relationships and social networks. The evidence suggests that women are more likely to have more supportive social networks than men following divorce or separation.

Religion

Many researchers point out that the increase in the rate of suicide is partly due to the decline in the popularity of religion. In the past, when religion had a much stronger influence on society, suicide was considered a major sin against God. People would not risk attracting the wrath of God by ending their own lives. They suffered on in silence, or took consolation in alcohol or whatever else they could find, to escape from their feelings of misery and despair. Religion gave people a sense of belonging, a link with God, meaning and purpose in their lives, light at the end of life's dark tunnels.

Cultural Factors

Medical research on emigrants from different European countries to both America and Australia has shown that for the next two generations, the suicide rates of the emigrants remained consistent with their country of origin. As the influence of the old culture diminished within these families, as they adopted the lifestyle of the country to which they had emigrated, the suicide rates within these families changed to the rates of their adopted country. People who feel isolated within their family, culture or community are far more likely to end their life than people who feel they belong.

Unemployment

The rate of suicide is higher in people without jobs. Society values people according to their job, their status, their income. Not having a job – especially for men – can be a severe blow. There are other knock-on effects of unemployment which create great strain for the un-employed person and his family, not least the financial implications of not having a steady income. Unemploy-ment is associated with loss of face and prestige. What is not taken into account is that the fundamental problem is often more than the lack of employment. The person's emotional vulnerability may make it too threatening to seek or to hold down a job. In the 'Celtic Tiger' Irish economy, there is less unemployment in Ireland than at any time in living memory. Yet the suicide rates in Ireland keep rising. Many of those who take their own lives have steady and well-paid jobs. It seems that employment status is an important factor but it is only one among many important human concerns which together add up to make a person feel that their life is worth living or not.

A study of teenagers aged thirteen and fourteen looked at what factors these teenagers felt might push them or their peers to suicide. Virtually all the answers were important social factors, rather than psychiatric illness:

- 49 per cent felt that the most common reason for suicide was linked to schools, examination pressures, bullying and intimidation.
- 35 per cent mentioned issues relating to their home life and family.
- 13 per cent felt that social isolation was an important trigger.
- 20 per cent said that depression was an important factor.

Young people – the age group most likely to take their own life – have a great deal more stress in their lives than perhaps we realise. A 1998 British survey commissioned by the *Bread for Life* campaign confirmed this. The protected environment in which children grew up twenty years ago has been replaced by a freer, less protected one. The range of issues young people have to deal with as they are growing up has greatly increased: peer-group pressure, friendship, parental expectation, family conflict, marital separation and divorce, bullying, sex, sexual orientation, eating disorders, alcohol, drugs, image, teenage pregnancy, finding suitable employment all exert pressure on young people. As they attempt to come to terms with these issues, many young people feel that they are not supported by their families.

Teenagers are searching for their identity as human

beings in their own right. The behaviour of teenagers is often motivated by a deep need to be accepted, to fit in with peers and to create some sense of independence from their family. Unfortunately, in many homes, teenage behaviour is interpreted as rebellion, and results in punishment and criticism. These parents may have misinterpreted the situation and in doing so they may have unwittingly heightened their child's sense of vulnerability and insecurity.

If we are really serious about reducing the suicide rate, we must concentrate our efforts on the needs of individuals. The family, and the relationships within the family, must become the cog around which suicide prevention stategies revolve. I believe that as long as psychiatry dominates the 'expert' platform, these issues will remain sidelined in favour of multi-million pound 'Fight Depression' (with drugs) campaigns which have never been shown to reduce the suicide rate. It sometimes seems that modern medicine presumes that the quality of a person's relationships with their family has no bearing on a person's suicide risk. Given how intense relationships can be, this is a dangerous presumption.

SUICIDE: A SANE ACT
To people contemplating suicide, ending their own life makes a great deal of sense. Suicide is not an act of insanity. The decision to end one's life is not the result of a sudden flick of a switch in the brain. At that moment of utter despair, suicide seems the only way to end the pain. Even when, to the outside world, the person's decision to kill themselves is inexplicable, I believe that

the person knows precisely why at that moment in their life, suicide seemed the right action. Until modern medicine wakes up to this, I believe that doctors will make little progress in their efforts to reduce the suicide rate.

According to the late GP and coroner Dr Bartley Sheehan in an interview in *The Irish Times*, 8 January 1991:

> Suicide is a response to the individual's perception of their circumstances and their experience. All of the perceptions that lead people to suicide are internal to the person. They are proper and appropriate perceptions. They are the individual standing in their own experience of their own lives. It may make no sense to you or to me or to anybody else, but it is their experience. And if one could be in touch with them about their experience, to hear and know what that experience was, one might well accept that the proper and appropriate thing for them to do would be for them to stop this experience, that it makes sense, in their circumstances, for them to take their own lives.

Dr Sheehan's views make sense to me. I believe he is accurately reflecting the inner world of people who take their own lives. But his views are not shared by the vast majority of doctors, who instead believe that the act of suicide is caused by 'mental illness' – the person was not in his 'right mind' when he ended his own life. Every individual who makes a serious suicide attempt is clear about one thing. They want their inner pain and turmoil to end. As they plan their suicide, they can see no other way out of their despair and hopelessness.

As the following case histories show, the determination of the majority of those who take their lives to proceed with the act strongly suggests that these individuals are very clear regarding what they are about to do.

Mary (see p 248) carefully planned her suicide attempt in advance. She travelled from Dublin to Galway so that she could throw herself into the river Corrib. Before jumping into the river, she calmly went for one last cup of coffee. She was very clear that she had had enough pain in her life. She saw suicide as her only way out.

Anne (see p 231) described what a sane act suicide is. When she reached the depths of despair, suicide entered her mind as a realistic way of ending her desperate emotional pain and suffering.

In the 1997 *Late Late Show* dedicated to suicide, several examples of carefully planned suicides were shared. A prison officer described the suicide of a prison inmate:

> He was in a cell, and what amazed me was the ingenuity of how he actually committed suicide. He was in a padded cell for his own protection; there was just a mattress and a blanket in it. Unfortunately, the glass was missing from a spyhole. He tore the cover off the mattress and made a knot. He shoved the knot out through the spyhole. There was a flap on the outside of

the spyhole. The flap came across, caught the knot and jammed it. He apparently just sat down behind the door, and that's the way he committed suicide. I had actually just checked on him myself, and a couple of minutes later it was brought to my attention that there was a knot sticking out through the spyhole. We went to check it out. We pushed the knot in, and we opened the door, and the poor chap fell out on top of us.

An article on teenage suicide in the *Irish Tatler* in April 1998 described how Paul carefully planned his suicide. He was clear about what he wanted to do. He chose the isolated woods of County Wicklow as the place. He travelled by bus from Dublin on the chosen day. He went to the trouble of bringing hundreds of paracetamol tablets and some alcohol. Paul felt very excited about ending his own life. As he travelled that day on the bus, he was caught up in the drama of what he was about to do, as if starring in a movie. He was not at all ambivalent as he prepared to end his life.

A study of suicides in Sweden found that four out of five people who end their lives make some sort of communication to one or more people about their intentions. Given the depth of their despair, this communication may not be clear. Its significance may be understood only after the person has ended their life. It therefore seems as if most people who take their own lives have pondered over this decision for some time. The decision is not an insane choice. They have had enough. They have to end their pain. Suicide, the ultimate act of avoidance, is the option which makes most sense. It seems most appropriate at that moment in their lives.

RELATIONSHIPS AND FAMILIES

> No man develops by himself: a person develops always in relationship with others. The relationships that most matter are those that occur within the family. It is now known that one person's ability to cope with life and another person's limited ability or inability to cope with life can be traced back to the pattern of relationships that operated within his family.
>
> Dr Tony Humphreys

According to Virginia Satir, American family therapist and author of *Peoplemaking*, a five-year-old child has already had about a billion interactions with other people, principally his or her parents. People who enter relationships or get married are expected to know how to handle difficulties and conflicts which frequently arise in their relationships on their own. Parents are expected to know instinctively how best to rear their children.

But parenting is the most difficult profession on earth. Parents receive little training or guidance. Many do not have support when the going gets tough. How we relate to other people is fundamentally important to our happiness and well-being. Yet we do not have a structured and easily accessible service to help people understand themselves, others, and improve their ability to communicate with others.

Because they usually look after the medical care of several members of the family, general practitioners are also known as 'family doctors'. Ironically, GPs receive little training in relationships and interpersonal communication. In my opinion, the medical profession does not sufficiently understand how relationships within the family can hurt – and heal. For the first fifteen to eighteen years of every person's life the relationships within the family are critically important. Relationships do make lasting impressions. Yet modern medicine does not devote any time or research to deepening its understanding of relationships. Here is a brief summary of the main relationships in a young person's life and how important they are to every human being:

The Family of Origin

Every person shares their early life with other people. We all had a father, a mother and perhaps brothers and sisters. Their presence – or their absence – plays a central part in our lives. Most children live at home until their late teens. Powerful and intense relationships between the child and the various members of the family have a huge influence on how they emerge from being a dependent child into adulthood. Even after a young adult leaves home to create their own life, relationships with parents and siblings remain very important.

Children need to feel safe, secure and supported at home, ideally by both parents. They need to feel loved unconditionally. They need to know that their parents' love for them will not be withdrawn under any circumstances. If a young person leaves their home of origin with high self-esteem, feeling safe enough to create their new life without being deeply threatened, they will usually want to maintain contact with their family of origin. The bond of love will ensure that keeping the family together remains high on their priority list, while at the same time they continue to carve out their own life, in their own way.

Young adults with low self-esteem may need to rely heavily on the family for support in a world which appears threatening. They may rebel and have little to do with their family. Often young adults do not feel they can communicate their true feelings and vulnerabilities within their family. Experience may have taught them that their family cannot hear what they need to say, cannot give them the emotional safety and support they desperately need.

I believe that, in general, parents do their best for their children, given the parents' own self-esteem, experience of life and sense of safety in the world. But I have come across many cases where the parents have been unable to meet the needs of their children. Parents are human beings, after all. Many parents were themselves reared in home environments where their emotional needs for safety, security, unconditional love and acceptance were not met. Consequently, many human beings do not feel safe in their lives. Feeling unsafe, parents react to life and people by protecting themselves. They feel they have to. Their emotional survival depends on it.

The critical relationships for a child are obviously those within the family of origin, in particular with parents. Parents' own need to protect themselves from hurt or criticism may prompt them to deal with the child in such a way that the child feels the parents' love has been withdrawn. The more often this happens, the more unsafe children feel, and the more coping mechanisms they develop – avoidance, overcompensating, not speaking their mind, competitiveness, anxiety, rebelling, aggression, passivity or perfectionism, to name just a few. It is important that young adults be encouraged to create their own life, to leave the nest. I have seen many families where the parents, owing to their own emotional vulnerabilities, have held on to their children well into their adult life. This situation can create huge emotional conflict and greatly reduce their offspring's ability to create a fulfilling life for themselves.

Low self-esteem is known to be linked with virtually every so-called 'mental illness' including depression, schizophrenia, alcohol abuse and drug abuse, the conditions most likely to precipitate suicide. Many researchers have found that low self-esteem is directly related to suicide. I believe that developing high self-esteem in our children is a most important preventative step society can take to reduce the suicide rate. Relationships – within the family but also in the child's wider world of school, neighbourhood and extended family – are the main influence on a child's level of self-esteem.

The Extended Family

Ideally, relationships with members of the extended family should feel safe and supportive. They should reinforce the child's sense of self-esteem and self-worth. Such extended family relationships are wonderful, a real blessing. Unfortunately, extended family relationships can have the opposite effect, undermining the person's already vulnerable sense of self-worth. Sometimes emotional, physical and sexual abuse occurs in relationships with extended family members. These relationships can have a devastating effect on a young person's life. Such invasion of the young person's life by an extended family member may occur when the parents do not see – or choose not to see – what is going on. They may be too stressed to hear or act on the appeals of their children to put a stop to the abuse.

Other Important Relationships in Our Early Lives
Young children have many important relationships outside of their own family. Many pre-school children spend a good deal of time in crèches or with minders. At four or five years of age, children begin their relationship with school and all that goes with it – relationships with teachers, other children, peer pressure, rules and regulations, schoolwork. As children grow older, they enter more relationships. Many social activities involve new relationships and new challenges. These new relationships and expectations can be far more threatening to young people than we adults sometimes realise.

The quality of the child-parent relationship affects relationships and situations outside the home. Some parents may not have sufficient self-esteem to stand up for the rights and feelings of their children – at school, with friends, with extended family members – even when they do know what is going on. If a child has a problem with a teacher, or is being bullied, or has an aunt who is very critical, they depend on the parent to resolve this conflict for them. Of course, there are times when the child needs to act on his own behalf. But he needs to know that his parents will act when he is unable to deal with the situation on his own.

If the parents do not hear the child's cry for help; if the parents do not or cannot take the necessary steps to find out precisely what the problem is and act to resolve it without delay; if the bullying continues; if the problem with the teacher continues; if the child's bombardment by a judgemental aunt continues, the child's self-esteem may be seriously undermined. The child may sense that those to whom they turn for safety are not providing enough protection. The child may then have to develop other protective strategies, designed to decrease the threat they feel: protective mechanisms such as anxiety, avoidance and withdrawal.

Relationships and the family are discussed in greater detail in other books. My intention here is to emphasise their importance and relevance to any discussion about emotional distress, 'mental illness' and suicide. Any assessment of the tragedy of suicide is incomplete without a thorough study of the family and relationships. Children need to receive clear messages from their parents about how unique and priceless they are. Unfortunately, many children are reared on a diet of criticism, judgement, put-down messages, and comparison with siblings or other young people. Because parents too need to protect themselves from showing their own vulnerability, many teenagers do not feel close to their parents.

Homes where teenagers can openly discuss all the issues which dominate their lives and which dominate their conversations with their friends – sex, contraception, love, the transition into adulthood, drugs, alcohol – are uncommon. Whatever intimacy children had with their parents in their earlier years tends to diminish during the teenage years. Many parents who fully believe they have a good relationship with their children do not realise that their children may be afraid to tell them things. Children know what they can tell their parents and what they cannot. The more personal issues they cannot discuss openly with their parents, the more of themselves they have to hide from the world and the more isolated, scared and lonely they feel. But parents may not be aware of what is going on within their children.

If children feel safe and loved unconditionally in their relationship with their parents, they are more likely to feel comfortable about bringing up whatever is bothering them. If they know they will get an open and com-passionate hearing, they are more likely to discuss issues with their parents. The parent will often not even need to ask – children will ask for help if they feel safe enough to do so. If the parent does ask questions, children will open up only if they know from previous experience of this relationship that it is safe to open up without fear of rejection, judgement or ridicule. Perhaps, too often, parents offer advice from their own perspective, rather than tuning in to their child's perspective of the situation or problem.

We find it difficult to cope and we survive by pre-tending that everything is all right. This came across strongly in *Boys Don't Cry*, a programme about suicide in young men broadcast in the *Panorama* strand on BBC 1 on 14 December 1998. A young man who had taken his own life was described by his male friends as a poser, a prankster – full of laughs. The interviewer asked them if he confided in them or spoke about his fears, his pain. From the bar-counter, pints in hand, they replied that he kept everything to himself. Appearing shocked by the very idea of confiding in others, his friends said that talking about yourself was not something you did with your mates, 'not with the lads'.

If people cannot talk about their feelings with their friends and they do not feel comfortable showing any vulnerability with their families, to whom can they turn? Speaking about the family of one young man who had taken his life, the presenter said:

> Like so many parents, this young man's parents thought they knew their son, but there were obviously things he felt he could not share with his parents.

I remember Philip, an eighteen-year-old who had been quiet and withdrawn throughout his teenage years. He lived within a loving family, but I felt that the dynamics of the interpersonal relationships within the family provided some clue. Philip's father was a dynamic, high-achieving businessman, to whom no problem was insurmountable. The home was run like a business venture. When Philip went to his father with problems, his father quickly responded with solutions and ideas. Unwittingly, Philip's father did not give Philip the chance to air his worries, explore them with his father, and find his own solutions. Being insecure and emotionally vulnerable, Philip was frightened by his father's apparent self-assuredness and decisiveness, and over the years responded by rarely going to his father any more with his problems. People can become isolated and withdrawn even when they live within a loving family.

The public and the medical profession need to realise that every person's own reality is valid for them. Whether it is hearing voices, becoming withdrawn, depressed, or highly anxious, what the person is experiencing must be accepted as valid for that person. A respectful exploration of that reality will frequently lead to a deeper understanding of what is going on for the person.

The stories of Eileen and Anne are two case histories of middle-aged women who found themselves on the brink of suicide. For these women, the central role that relationships and life events played in bringing them both to the point of self-destruction is self-evident in their stories, as is the failure of the medical profession to offer meaningful help.

EILEEN'S STORY

Eileen's life story demonstrates the devastating effects troubled family relationships can have on people: effects which can permeate into the person's adult life. Eileen has felt lonely and unloved throughout her life. When she sought help from the medical profession for her emotional distress, the 'help' she received actually pushed her closer to suicide. Given how typical her story is of the lives of countless thousands, I asked her to write her story in her own words:

I am a forty-year-old married woman and mother of two wonderful children. A few years ago, I could have been lost to them forever. I tried to take my own life with a cocktail of pills that were supposed to cure all my problems. From my experience, GPs who are too busy or who don't take time to listen and just dish out pills to get rid of you have a lot to answer for. They treat the symptoms and ignore the real cause.

Psychiatrists are wrong to label everyone who takes their own life as mentally ill. Babies are not born with a psychiatric illness, but I do believe that, when pushed to the limit of endurance, everyone has a breaking point when they just can't take any more pain, hurt, disappointment, loss, sorrow, worry, anxiety, fear, pressure, stress, mental and physical abuse, insults, humiliation, being demoralised, living in poverty and debt, and as a result ending up with so many health symptoms that their GP starts ignoring them and treats them as if they were a hypochondriac.

I had contemplated ending my life many times. Five years ago, I almost succeeded in taking my life when the behaviour of one family member finally drove me over the edge. I was once again reduced to tears, and I decided I couldn't take any more of this life. I had lost my identity as a human being and I just couldn't cope any more. It was as if I was on a merry-go-round and couldn't get off. I had absolutely no quality of life and – it seemed to me then – no hope of regaining any. It wasn't an attention-seeking gesture, as my GP later told my son – I was furious when I heard that. I took enough tablets to make sure I wouldn't survive and locked my door to prevent anyone from finding me in time.

I didn't leave any notes. I didn't show any hints – that I am aware of – to anyone about what I was going to do. As it happened, one of my sons came home unexpectedly and came looking for me. Otherwise I would have died. People say that suicide is a coward's way out, but I believe it takes courage to do what I did. At that moment, I felt I was doing my family a favour. People also say that suicide is a selfish act. I certainly didn't feel selfish at that moment. I felt the complete opposite. I felt they'd all be better off without a useless and dysfunctional mother.

I'm a middle-aged woman now, and my life has been made up of losses, rejections, being used and abused physically and mentally. I realised at a very young age that my parents were bad-tempered and violent. I tried to protect my siblings by always taking the blame and being severely punished for the little incidents of childhood, like breaking a cup. No matter who did the wrong, I took the blame to save them from being battered until pain was experienced or blood was drawn, usually from the legs. So the pattern developed that I either got blamed for every wrong, or I took the blame myself.

I was raped when I was sixteen years old by a family friend, a well-known and respected member of the community. Because I didn't feel loved by my parents, I couldn't tell them. For years after the rape, I was burdened with guilt, believing I was somehow to blame for it. When your self-esteem is so low and your need to be loved is so great, you cling to anyone for affection and don't realise until it is too late that you are being used – not loved. I'm not a bad person. All my life I have loved too much, given of myself too much, both emotionally and physically. I have been over-generous with my time and dedication to family and others.

By my late thirties I was well and truly burnt out. I had nothing left to give, but I was still expected to keep on giving because there was no one to step into my shoes. Looking back now, I moved from an abused, traumatic and fearful childhood into marriage at a very young age. I married young to escape from home. But unfortunately, I married a man who was very insecure and immature, who was and still is suffering the effects of a neglected, insecure childhood, which he will not acknowledge. We both carried baggage into our marriage, which was a disaster from day one. That was twenty years ago, and I'm literally crying inside ever since.

By the time I was thirty-one years old I had lost six people who were close and dear to me, five of whom died young – three very close friends, my favourite uncle, my sister, and my grandfather, whom I loved very much. My husband never really married me in the true sense of the word. He always remained tied to his mother's apron strings. He was rarely there for me when I needed him but he was always there for his mother. I raised my children on my own and during the many bereavements I had in my life, he was never there for me. When I miscarried two pregnancies, one after the other, he screamed at me to shut up whimpering so that he could get to sleep. He spent his life either in the pubs or in bed, sleeping off the effect of the drink.

As the mother of young children, I had to go out to work when the children were very small to pay off the huge debts incurred by my husband's total lack of responsibility to his wife and children. Because we lived in relative poverty and had huge debts, I was constantly trying to work outside the home and still be at home enough to rear my children and keep the house clean. This left me working eighteen to twenty hours a day with little or no time to eat properly, and certainly no time for me.

My GP didn't have time to listen to the real cause of my problems and just kept throwing more and more pills at me. He stopped listening to me, and treated me as if I was a hypochondriac. I became very aware that I was being ignored by my GP and I became very frustrated and depressed because I was feeling worse rather than better. The medication I was on made me feel like a zombie. I was taking diazepam [a tranquilliser], Prozac [an antidepressant], Prothiadin [another antidepressant], and Rohypnol [a sleeping tablet] all at the same time, along with other medication. I was like a walking chemist shop. As a result of all this medication, my speech became slurred and I was incoherent. My concentration was gone and my memory was seriously impaired.

Getting worse, I just couldn't cope any more. I was felt so empty inside, I couldn't see any future. Everything seemed so hopeless, so black, no way out. That was when I attempted suicide. I believe the medication I was on which was supposed to improve how I felt – the antidepressants, tranquillizers and sleeping tablets – actually contributed to my reaching the point of suicide, because I felt like a zombie. And because the best that the doctors could offer was actually making me worse, I lost all hope of improvement. Psychiatrists may say what they like, but let any one of them be subjected to all I was subjected to all my life and see if they wouldn't crack under unrelenting torture of many kinds.

I believe that people take or attempt to take their lives when they cannot endure any more pain. The emotional pain of bashing their heads off a brick wall in a desperate effort to bring some kind of normality into the adverse circumstances that life and other people led them into – either by force, fear, threat, condemnation, rejection, jealousy, subservience or whatever.

After my suicide attempt, I decided to take control of my own health. I changed doctors and insisted on getting the proper tests and treatments which were necessary for my medical conditions. I'm no longer a pushover in the doctor's surgery. I haven't swallowed a pill for two years – which makes me wonder if I ever really needed the seven different medications I was taking every day for years before my suicide attempt. I jumped off the medication roller coaster. I dumped all the pills down the loo and I started to live again. I am and always have been sane and at last I am enjoying my children. I am just a human being whose emotional needs were never met – not in my childhood, and certainly not in my marriage.

'Mental illness' was not the cause of Eileen's suicide attempt. Eileen became distraught because her emotional needs were not met in her life – her need to feel loved, to feel close to her parents in her early life and later to her husband. The failure of these relationships to meet

230

her needs for love, support and affirmation left her very insecure and consumed with self-doubt. I believe it is a travesty of natural justice that people such as Eileen are labelled 'mentally ill'. Having lived a series of disappointments and put-downs, Eileen was again put down by the medical profession to whom she turned for help.

Children's development into self-assured and confident adulthood is facilitated if the important adults in their lives – parents particularly – demonstrate in word and deed that they love their children deeply. Since children often see themselves as they think their parents see them, parents need to communicate to their children that they matter; that the parents believe in, respect and trust their children. Children need to be affirmed as important, unique human beings. Parents frequently presume that their children know they love and believe in them. This love and belief needs to be demonstrated to children. Otherwise they may have to try to read their parents' minds.

ANNE'S STORY

Now forty years old, Anne has felt suicidal on many occasions. The eldest of five children, she grew up in the suburbs of Limerick city. She was reared in a family which to the outside world was normal, caring and respectable, a high-profile family in the community. But within the four walls of the family home, it was a different story. Love was rarely shown. The children were emotionally and physically abused by parents who were themselves emotionally vulnerable. Anne never felt close to anyone during her childhood. When Anne was only three years old, she sensed her mother's deep emotional vulnerability. She felt, even at that tender age, that her mother could not be there for her. When Anne was eight years old, she was sent by her parents to live with elderly relations. Anne was the only child in that house and she did not get on with her surrogate parents.

She became intensely lonely and felt abandoned by her parents. She begged her parents to take her back, but they refused. Hers was not a family where feelings were discussed. Anne kept her intense emotional pain to herself. So intense was her pain that for years she had to suppress any awareness of how seriously dysfunctional her family was. All her siblings were also deeply affected.

In her own words, Anne describes her experience of anxiety and depression, and how close she came to taking her own life. Anne's suicidal feelings were not caused by 'mental illness' but by loneliness, relationship conflicts and low self-esteem. Her life experiences resemble those of many people who are labelled 'mentally ill.' I felt that people who have gone through similar life experiences would identify with Anne's, so I asked Anne to write her own story:

> Some experiences defy accurate description. I believe that being in a suicidal state within yourself is one of those experiences. The pain is so deep, it occurs at a level where words don't apply. Words such as hopelessness, despair, black, and abyss all come to mind, but they only touch at the edges of this awful place. For me, no words come close to reaching the core of this

profound and unbearable pain. Having said that, I will try as best I can to describe what was going on for me at those times, and what brought me on many occasions to the point of self-destruction.

Having come from a highly neglectful, painful and deeply rejecting childhood, I came into adulthood hating myself, and with a deep sense of feeling inferior to everyone. I felt worthless and invisible, unloved and totally unlovable. I felt it was even wrong to allow myself to be loved. I was deeply insecure and dependent on others. How I saw myself fed into every area of my life – my family, my workplace, my relationships, and my social life. In order to protect myself from feeling the pain of hurt, rejection and abandonment, and deep, deep sadness, I spent all my time avoiding situations where I might be hurt or rejected. Instead, I spent my life caring for others. I went into extreme perfectionism in my life and in my job.

I was breaking up inside, while outside I kept smiling and pretending that all was well. That I felt it absolutely necessary to keep all this pain to myself and hide what was really going on inside me from my family and friends brought me into a place of great loneliness and emotional isolation. Eventually my body broke down and I became seriously ill. I felt that my family were totally unable to cope with my life-threatening illness. They couldn't even talk about what was happening to me. I don't blame them for this. I am now coming to a place of compassion and understanding for them. I know they had to react in this way in order to cope with my illness.

But the pressure of bottling up what I was feeling any longer – and hiding the terror of a life-threatening illness – was becoming too much to bear. I experienced acute anxiety symptoms on a daily basis and my health continued to deteriorate. I wanted to die. Everything I did took an enormous amount of energy out of me. My anxiety became chronic and was accompanied by terror, daily panic attacks and depression.

My life had by now lost all sense of meaning and normality. I had become addicted to tranquillizers and sleeping tablets. I had lost my health and my sense of independence. I was still struggling with many painful emotional issues. Worst of all, I had lost all peace of mind. There were times I felt I was going mad. I craved understanding for the pain I was in, but emotionally, I felt I was in a desert. To talk from the heart, to feel, to trust, to be real in our family could not be faced or even discussed. That was how we lived. But for me, the pressure of pretence had become too great. There is a point of emotional pain beyond which a person cannot endure, and I had reached that point. I became hopeless. I saw no hope that things could ever change. I woke every morning into a nightmare of hopelessness, oppression and terror about how I would cope with my pain, and the aloneness and pressure I felt trying to hide it constantly from those around me.

I was in a black hole of total darkness within myself. It was too painful to stay in that black hole of despair, but I couldn't see any way out. I couldn't see any future. Many times, I did not live from day to day. I just held on from hour to hour, not knowing for how long more I could endure the pain. Now I knew what despair was. I wanted to kill myself. It was the only way out. On more than one occasion, when I planned out how I would take my life, I silently said 'goodbye' to a young niece of mine whom I dearly loved. Nothing can describe the utter isolation I felt on those occasions. But to reach out and say what was going on for me risked more rejection, more abandonment. And that was more than I could take. The only way left for me was to end it all. Suicide is tragic, yes, but it is a wise and sane action – the ultimate act of avoidance of any further pain.

What the medical profession offered didn't work for me. I attended seven doctors: three GPs, one psychiatrist and three other specialists. Without listening to what was going on for me at a deep emotional level, the three GPs, the psychiatrist, and most of the other specialists were telling me that there was a 'biochemical abnormality' in my brain which was causing my depression and that I needed antidepressants. I was carrying such a great weight of pain and I had reached such a low point in my life that I wanted to end it all. The last thing I needed was to be told that there was something 'wrong' with me. That drove me deeper into hopelessness. I remember clearly rushing home to ring my therapist after one such consultation with a doctor, just to hear her tell me that there was nothing 'wrong' with me. I felt so distressed that evening that if I hadn't had my therapist's reassurance, the preceding consultation with a doctor could well have been the last straw that might have broken me.

As I already mentioned, I attended a psychiatrist on one occasion. That consultation lasted thirty minutes. I remember feeling during our conversation 'he doesn't really know what emotional pain is like'. I desperately needed to feel empathy from that psychiatrist, but I didn't feel any. I knew halfway through our interaction what the outcome would be, and I was right. He spoke of chemical disorders in my brain and the need for antidepressant drug treatment. Once again I felt misunderstood, flawed and hopeless at hearing that a chemical in my brain was the cause of my deep feelings of pain, loss and emotional isolation. But I would have tried anything to ease the pain, so I started taking antidepressants.

Then began a further nightmare of trying one antidepressant after another. Each produced intolerable side effects, from intense agitation and feelings of unreality to violent headaches. Yet none of these drugs gave me any sense of well-being or peace. Antidepressants, my last resort, the thrust of the recommended treatment by the medical experts, had failed.

The medical profession and psychiatry need to look seriously at how they view the people who come to them with deep emotional issues. These are life-and-death situations. These are people who are fragile and very vulnerable at that moment in their life. To merely look at a set of symptoms and not look behind them to see what is causing them is not good enough. To send people away after a ten- or twenty-minute consultation with a box of tablets and a message about a chemical disorder can mean the end of the road for some people, the last straw. I know that if I had not gone on a different road, to seek another way of healing, I would not be here today. On many occasions, I left my family home not knowing whether I would ever return. I remember one Sunday evening, I knew I had to get out of my home. I told my family I was going to Mass. Somewhere in me, I felt that if I got into the car, I wouldn't ever come back. As I left my home, something made me turn left, instead of the usual right turn onto the main road. I went to visit Joan, an acquaintance who lived nearby. At that time we barely knew each other.

I poured out my heart to her and instantly I knew she understood. She spent more than three hours hearing me, and being with me, in my deep suicidal distress. That was two years ago, and since then Joan's love, her empathy, caring and support have known no bounds. I have indeed been inspired and healed by her. I now know that only love heals. In recent years I have been blessed to have a deeply compassionate therapist in my life. She is the person who has saved my life, and has changed it forever. Without her enduring unconditional loving acceptance of me over the past number of years, I feel I would either have wasted away – because I didn't care whether I lived or died – or I would have ended my agony by suicide.

I knew her love for me was always there. But sometimes I would lose sight of that love, and these were the blackest moments of all. These were the times I came closest to ending up in the river. During those 'nightmares' I would sometimes get a fleeting glimpse of that unconditional compassionate love. And that would be the turning point for me. I would break down and cry uncontrollably, thanking God that I had not ended it all. For I had felt again the depth of my therapist's understanding love, and that had stopped me from going over the brink.

In fact, I have been thrice blessed, because fifteen months ago, Terry Lynch, my present GP came into my life. He has a deep understanding of human behaviour and healing. His caring and support for me have known no limits. There were many days when, before a consultation with Terry, I wanted to end it all. But after the consultation, because I knew he had heard me, cared for me, and connected with me in my place of total despair, my aloneness would lift. I would again feel it was worth hanging on in there.

Some time ago, when I was going through a particularly bleak and despairing time, what held me in there over the weekend was knowing that for Saturday and Sunday Terry had given me a time at which I could ring him and talk. On both of those days, I clearly remember that the only thing which gave me hope and kept me from giving up was knowing that at some stage during the day I could connect with someone who cared about me, who deeply understood my pain. That proves to me that love saves lives.

The love I have experienced in these three relationships is a love that has no strings attached. It is a love that loves me for myself unconditionally, no matter what I do, say or feel. It is a love that meets me in my pain, and understands me in my loneliness. It is a love that sees and hears me. When I am in deep despair, I cannot see beyond the pain. What helps me during those awful times is not tablets or solutions, but to be met by another person in that painful place, and to feel they understand what that place is like. Then the despair lifts, and I can move on. It is also a love that sees the 'rightness' of where I am, at that moment in my life. It is a love that believes in me and empowers me and is helping me to see myself as a person worthy of receiving and giving love. I would like to finish with a few lines from Brendan Kennelly:

Though we live in a world that dreams of ending,
That always seems about to give in,
'Something' that will not acknowledge conclusion,
Insists that we forever begin, begin, begin. . .

For me, that 'something' is hope, for without hope, we cannot feel, and without feeling, we cannot feel love. Without the love I have received in these three relationships, I would not be here today to tell my story.

Within her own family, Anne had always felt desperately alone. Like many a family, hers was one where you can talk about many things – the weather, the match, the neighbours, politics, TV programmes. But you do not talk about your feelings, your real worries, your human vulnerabilities. If she did talk about these sensitive issues, she was quickly silenced. She learned to keep her feelings and her thoughts to herself. She has often said to me that she feels far closer to her five-year-old niece than to either her parents or her five siblings. Prior to meeting me, Anne had attended seven doctors. Each doctor diagnosed depression and recommended antidepressants. None of them explored her childhood, her family life, her low self-esteem, her feelings. Not one of these seven doctors connected with her in her despair.

Anne says that the most important healing force in her recovery was not antidepressants, not tranquillizers, not a diagnosis. It was love – the love she felt from her therapist, from me, and from one wonderful friend. In these three relationships, Anne knew she mattered. Her uniqueness and pricelessness as a human being was repeatedly affirmed in these relationships. Consequently she has begun to reconnect with society, to create a life for herself which has meaning and fulfilment. This is really not so surprising. Love does heal, yet few doctors understand the immense healing power of compassion and caring. Love as a healing force isn't much mentioned in medical textbooks. Yet if doctors were more com-passionate, and better listeners, I believe there would be far less need for prescription drugs such as antidepres-sants and tranquillizers – and possibly far fewer suicides.

What was the 'love' which was so central to Anne's recovery? It was all the things she desperately needed as a child in her own home, but which her parents were themselves too vulnerable and hurt to give to her – unconditional acceptance; permission to express herself; safe relationships where she would not be judged, criti-cised, rejected, ridiculed or abandoned.

Many doctors become uncomfortable when patients show

their feelings. Crying is an important release of emotions that need to be expressed. But when patients cry in doctors' surgeries, the doctor's response is often to reach for the prescription pad. Whatever about the patient needing the prescription, the doctor frequently has a deep need to write one. The prescription is a swift way to stop the expression of emotion and end the consultation.

Doctors greatly underestimate the effect on people when they tell patients that their depression is a biochemical brain disorder. That no proof exists to back this up makes it all the more disconcerting. For Anne, being told she was suffering from a biochemical brain imbalance drove her even further into despair, and close to taking her own life.

As Anne says, I have been her GP for the past year and a half. However, I have not been providing Anne with a typical GP-type service. Most GPs would have treated Anne like the previous three GPs she came in contact with – a diagnosis and a prescription. I took a different approach. I focused on creating a deep, trusting relationship with Anne, where she felt important and cared for. Our relationship became much more like a deep friendship between two human beings than a doctor-patient relationship. Perhaps the medical profession has underestimated the most important part of the doctor-patient interaction – the relationship itself.

Frequently, when people attend both a therapist and a GP they get conflicting messages. The therapist says the emotional distress is caused by emotional, psychological or relationship issues, while the doctor says the cause is a brain chemical imbalance. The therapist believes that listening and talking is the best therapy. The doctor advises that drug therapy is best. These confusing messages create doubt in the patient's mind, often undermining their recovery. This did not happen in Anne's case, because I adopted the same approach as her therapist. Anne's recovery was speeded up because she was getting the same consistent message from me and from her therapist.

It is sad that in our society there is still such stigma around 'mental illness' and suicide. I have heard many stories from people recently discharged from psychiatric hospitals of how people avoid them, often crossing the street to escape meeting them. It is also sad that it is still not OK to talk openly about attempted suicide. When Michael attempted to take his life, his family gathered into a huddle to discuss what they would say to neighbours and friends. They agreed to say that Michael had had an accident. His family did not want the shame of an attempted suicide visited upon them within the community. Such defensiveness is common, and reflects the judgemental and prying attitude which still pervades modern Irish society. Given how eager people are to judge, I could see their point.

SELF-ESTEEM: A KEY ISSUE

How people feel about themselves has a huge bearing on their lives, including their likelihood of committing suicide. I believe that doctors greatly underestimate the importance of low self-esteem, mistakenly seeing it as the result – rather than a possible cause – of the psychiatric illness they are in the process of diagnosing.

In the *Journal of American Academic Child and Adoles-*

cent Psychiatry in July 1995, psychiatrist Dr J. Overholser
and his colleagues outlined their research paper which
highlighted the link between low self-esteem and suicide:

> Self-esteem can have a profound influence on a
> person's thinking, emotions and responses to
> stressful life events. Both suicidal ideation
> [thinking about suicide] and suicide attempts
> may be related to persistent negative views of
> the self. A negative view of the self may involve
> seeing the self as worthless, and the future as
> hopeless. The adolescent with low self-esteem
> may see life as not worth living and may
> perceive everyday stressors as overwhelming.
> Thus self-esteem deficits appear to be directly
> related to suicidal tendencies in adolescents.
>
> Low self-esteem may indirectly heighten the
> risk of suicidal behaviour by increasing a person's
> vulnerability to depression. The presence of
> depression is associated with increased risk of
> suicidal ideation, attempts, and completion. The
> tendency to see oneself as weak, inadequate and
> a failure is clearly related to depressed mood. Low
> self-esteem has been found to be closely related
> to depression in child psychiatric patients, adult
> psychiatric patients, and college student samples.
> Also, a strong association has been found
> between depression severity and low self-esteem
> in adolescent psychiatric inpatients, with
> improvement in depression coinciding with
> increases in self-esteem.

The authors of this paper highlight how little research has been done by psychiatry in the area of self-esteem:

> Despite the potentially important role of self-esteem in suicide risk among adolescents, few studies have directly examined the role of self-esteem in depression and suicidal behaviour among adolescents. Most research on self-esteem defects has been limited to larger studies of depression that includes self-esteem as a minor part of the study.

The researchers concluded:

> Treatment of depressed and suicidal adolescents should address the self-esteem deficits that may underlie these emotional problems.

Here is a psychiatrist stating that both depression and suicide are emotional rather than psychiatric problems. Yet mainstream psychiatry seeks to establish that these are primarily psychiatric problems, which in the eyes of the medical profession usually means physical brain defects. Why? Because psychiatry's very survival could depend on proving that so-called 'psychiatric illness' has a physical explanation, be it genetic or biochemical?

For years I have noticed a strong link between low self-esteem and depression. I believe that low self-esteem is a key issue in depression and in all 'psychiatric illnesses'. Dr Oalosaari, Dr Aro and Dr Laippala of the University of

Tampere in Finland published their study on parental divorce and depression in young adults in the medical journal *Acta Psychiatr Scandinavia* in 1996. Low self-esteem was shown to be a predictor of subsequent depression in young adults, regardless of their family background or gender.

In recent years, parents have become aware of the key importance of fostering self-esteem in their children. But parents receive little guidance in this regard. This is partly because psychiatry – rather than psychology – dominates the field of mental health, and psychiatrists under-estimate how important self-esteem really is. No suicide prevention programme will be successful unless self-esteem is a key topic within that programme.

7

THE MEDICAL PROFESSION'S APPROACH TO SUICIDE

In 1992, the British government set out to reduce the suicide rate by 33 per cent in those with psychiatric illness and by 15 per cent in the general population by the year 2000. The opposite has occurred in the past decade. The suicide rate has been increasing steadily in both Britain and Ireland during the past ten years.

DOES MODERN MEDICINE PREVENT SUICIDE?

Most medical experts believe that suicide is almost always caused by psychiatric illness. Despite the supposed expertise of modern medicine, no evidence exists to demonstrate that the interventions of the medical profession reduce the suicide rate.

People who have been in-patients in psychiatric hospitals have received the best that psychiatry has to offer. Yet they are more likely – not less, as you might expect – to kill themselves after discharge. Another group with a particularly high risk of taking their own lives are those who have previously attempted suicide. Most hospitals in westernised countries have a policy regarding people who attempt suicide. Once out of danger of dying from their suicide attempt, they are assessed by a psychiatrist. Appropriate follow-up psychiatric care is arranged once they are discharged. This is now standard practice. Psychiatry has established contact with both of these high suicide-risk groups. Both receive the best treatments that psychiatry has to offer. But their treatments are not working – indeed, they may be counter-productive.

Some people treated with drugs for depression in hospital take their own life within weeks of the commencement of treatment. Psychiatrists say this occurs because, as they improve, they gain enough energy to go about ending it all. This view ignores other explanations which are unpalatable to the medical profession:

- The social stigma of having been admitted to a psychiatric ward causes upheaval in the person's life.
- The increased hopelessness and isolation people feel when they are not listened to, when instead they are told to keep taking the tablets.
- The humiliating experience of a psychiatric admission creating within the person the conviction that they would rather die than risk having to go through that trauma again. Many recently discharged patients feel that they are sent home with little or no follow-up. They are sent home to pick up the pieces pretty much on their own.

Mary's Story

The following is the transcript of a live interview broadcast on RTE Radio on the *Pat Kenny Show* in 1998. Suicide was highly topical at the time. Mary was interviewed by Emer Woodful, referred to hereafter as EW:

EW: We have had many, many calls about suicide over the past few days and Mary is one of those. Good morning to you, Mary.

M: Good morning, Emer.

EW: What would you like to say to us?

M: It's twenty years this year since I was first admitted to a psychiatric hospital, and I have been admitted countless times to psychiatric hospitals, and I have made a few attempts on my life, and one very serious one, and therefore I think I am qualified to say something on the topic. And what strikes me is that every time there's a programme done, or a feature on suicide, an eminent psychiatrist is wheeled out to speak expertly on the subject. And in my experience psychiatry in its present form (even though there are good things about it, and there are good psychiatrists), psychiatry in general, in its present form contributes to suicide instead of lowering the rate. That's my own opinion.

EW: In what way, Mary?

M: Well, the most important quality that I would look for in a psychiatrist is a willingness to listen, to understand, to empathise, and not, *not* an over-readiness to diagnose, categorise, and reduce the person to a label, which is stamped on them, and once it is stamped on them, reduces if not eliminates their possibilities of employment or social life thereafter, and once labelled and categorised and put on disability benefit (if they've no other income) then they have the added stress of living on approximately seventy pounds a week plus perhaps rent allowance, suffering the scorn of community welfare officers, psychiatric nurses, and everybody in general. Because once you are reduced to that state, you have no social standing. You have no money, and you are known to be 'mental'. Then everybody heaps scorn upon you and what you are. And what you were is completely lost forever unless somebody remarkable realises it.

EW: What was your life like, Mary, that you felt so bad about your life that you wanted to die?

M: Well, at the time that I jumped twenty

feet into a raging torrent – it was in March, and it was after midnight, and it was on a cold night, and it was completely dark except for a moon out, and there was nobody about, and I stood for two hours, and I had to talk myself into jumping into that river, and by God knows what – providence – I was washed up against a weir, and I chose to climb out. And this is another point – I'll go into the question you asked me in a minute – but this a point I'd like to make. A researcher who was on the *Late Late Show*, and he was talking about a study he had done in Cork on suicide, and he noted that people who commit suicide, if at a certain point after they've taken the poison, or kicked the chair from under them, or jumped into the water, if they could turn the clock back, inevitably, they all would.

And the point is that, it is not that people want to die – and I'm not glamorizing suicide by saying this – it takes immense courage to take your own life. It's not that a person wants to die, it's that they cannot cope with life. And I suppose what made me take that jump was the utter belief that my life as it was then, packing meals in an industrial therapy unit, and living in a group home where every moment of your life was accounted for, and being totally cut off from everyday life, from – as they say – normal society and that. The absolute and utter belief that nothing would ever change. I remember saying to myself: 'Nobody will ever love me, I will never have children, I will never work.' And I kept repeating those things to myself until I made myself jump in.

EW: So you were looking down a really dark tunnel.

M: Yes. And as I jumped into the water I cried out, 'God forgive me, God forgive me!' because I knew that what I was doing was wrong.

EW: And what age were you, Mary, when you did this?

M: That was eleven years ago, so I would have been twenty-seven, twenty-eight.

EW: And what was your life like up to that point that you had fallen so low in your own life, and in your own feelings of worthlessness?

M: Well, my first admission to a [psychiatric] hospital was prior to my going to university, and while I was at university I had several admissions to hospital, and despite that I struggled on. But in the first job, which wasn't actually a

job, it was really a temporary place-
ment, I again became 'ill' in inverted
commas and was admitted to hospital.
And then the following year I got on to
a publishing course in Dublin and again
became 'ill'. And the following year I
just sort of 'slid' through. And the
following year I fell madly in love – with
somebody who fell madly in love with
me – for the first time in my life, and
became 'ill' and he just, virtually, didn't
want to know me any more.

And then I found myself living in
a group home. And that's when I. . . it
was quite a calm, almost a casual
decision, you know. It just kind of
occurred to me one day as I was going
down to meet one of these people who
reviews your entitlement to your
disability. And I thought, 'There will be
a bus to Galway at such-and-such a
time, and I could get on it, and I could
go to Galway and drown myself in the
river Corrib.' Because I thought, 'Well, if
I'm going to do it, I'd better make sure
that I do it properly, otherwise they [the
psychiatrists] will lock me up for good.'

And that's what I did, and I got on
the bus, and all the way to Galway I
kept repeating to myself, I said 'I have
to do this, I have to do this, I have to

do this.' And then when I got to Galway I even went into a coffee shop and sat down and had a cup of coffee. And then I walked over and went down past the cathedral, and down by Nun's Bridge, and into a spot which I had actually often chosen when I was a student, you know, tried to convince myself to jump in before that. And I stood there for two hours. And then I thought, well, in case they don't find my body, I'd better leave a note, so I left some of my belongings and a note there. And then I just stepped up on the railings and jumped in.

EW: And then what made you grab on to that weir?

M: Well, I didn't grab on to it, I actually. . . when I was in the water, I went right down and I was so relaxed, I wasn't frightened at all. I was just so peaceful and I was waiting to die, and I thought, 'in a few seconds it'll all be over.' And I felt completely at ease, and perhaps that's what saved my life, because they say if you struggle in the water, you'll drown quicker. And I just sank in to the water, and I heard this roaring in my ears, and I thought, 'Oh, that must be what people who are dying experience.' And then I felt something like metal against my neck, then a sort of a fern brushed my cheek.

And then suddenly my head was above the water and I was looking at the moon, and I was confused. I thought, 'I'm not dead yet' and I was puzzled for a while. Then I realised my skirt was so saturated with water that it was pinning me against... I don't understand it, it's where they change the level of water. I was pinned against this weir, or whatever it is that adjusts the water level, and I looked about me for a while, and I thought, 'Will I wait here until the water rises to the level to cover my head, or will I get up and jump in again?'

Then I thought, sort of half-heartedly, 'Well, maybe it's not so bad after all' and then there were some bars there so I just pulled myself up. I got up and got on to the bank – and this is the funny part actually, because I went to the nearest house and knocked on the door. And when the woman opened, because it was rag week that week, she thought it was a prank by some student, and she slammed the door in my face!! [laughing]

EW: Oh dear!

M: I suppose I can afford to laugh now,

because I feel safe, I feel safe, I feel as if I've distanced myself sufficiently from it that I can look back now and even though I can realise the horror of it, I can see the funny parts as well.

EW: And, Mary, what has helped you move into a space that you feel is obviously a much safer one?

M: Well, the single factor is a relationship with a man whom I met in a psychiatric hospital, and I don't know why, but he understands me as well or even better than I understand myself, and des-pite. . . I mean he has seen me ill, he has seen me in all my varying moods and whatever, and he loves me. I mean, that's the only word I can use, and accepts me for what I am, and sees the potential in me because – that's another point – a lot of the potential of psychiatric patients is completely lost and smothered by the concentration on their illness. I don't know who said it about 'great men and madness do near a-lie, and thin partitions do them divide'. And there are a lot of im-mensely talented people whose talent is completely burnt up and wasted in psychiatric hospitals. And it has not been a smooth path by any manner of means. We've had a terrible, terrible struggle together. And we're still struggling but we're still together – touch wood. If you're in adverse circumstances together, if you're thrown together early, in adverse circumstances, then that proves a relationship, really.

EW: Definitely. And what is your life like now, Mary?

M: Well, by most people's standards it's very dull, it would seem very dull. I cannot work because I'm classed as disabled because of all the years of illness. I live in a rented house which we did up ourselves, and I take great pleasure in just the whole idea of having a place that you can paint your own colours and hang your own pictures, and that sort of thing, and I actually enjoy life probably more than if I was slotted into a job. I still have huge ambitions, and I think that's what keeps me going.

EW: Well, listen, thanks very much for calling us this morning, and look after yourselves!

M: Oh don't worry, I'm well looked after!

EW: Good! All right Mary, Thanks very much for that, thank you, all right, bye-bye. . .

When it comes to understanding suicide, Mary had the edge on the psychiatric experts. Unlike most psychiatrists, Mary had personal experience of reaching such a level of despair and hopelessness that suicide seemed the only way out. It is clear from the interview that Mary had been on the receiving end of psychiatric care for many years of her life. She had a pretty thorough understanding of the psychiatric system, and what it is like to be a psychiatric patient.

Might Modern Medicine Contribute to Suicide?

Psychiatry does not emerge well from this interview with Mary. As she said, every time suicide is featured in the media, an eminent psychiatrist is wheeled out to speak expertly on the topic. This practice reinforces the view that psychiatrists are the experts when it comes to suicide, that psychiatry is the field of study most likely to solve the tragedy of suicide. Mary was clearly not happy about this. It is the first point she makes and may well be why she contacted the programme in the first place. Mary believed that rather than helping to lower the rate of suicide, psychiatry in its present form actually contributes to suicide. Not only was Mary speaking from years of personal experience of and exposure to psychiatry, but through her years of attending psychiatric hospitals she would have come to know many other psychiatric patients and would have seen how they were treated.

I too believe that psychiatry contributes to suicide. The last thing a person in the depths of despair needs is a system which labels rather than listens. In the interview,

Mary speaks about the qualities she believes psychiatrists should possess:

> a willingness to listen, to understand, to empathise, and not, *not* an over-readiness to diagnose, to categorise, to reduce a person to a label.

It appears that she frequently felt her psychiatrists did not listen, did not understand or empathise with her but were over-ready to diagnose, to categorise her. Perhaps Mary's experience gives us a clue to why people discharged from psychiatric wards are at a greatly increased risk of suicide.

Mary eloquently describes the stigma of psychiatric labelling: reduced or eliminated social life and employment opportunities; poverty; increased social isolation and public scorn, including at times the scorn of those who are part of the psychiatric care team. She makes many points that should be studied very carefully by those involved in the care of the hurt and the vulnerable, none more important than the following:

> It is not that people want to die, it's that they cannot cope with life.

People take their lives because they have reached the point where the only way they can see to end their despair and pain is to end their existence.

When the person reaches such a low point that they are seriously thinking of taking their own life, it has already become almost impossible for them to reach out for help. If they do reach out one more time, it is crucial that they are – as Mary said – listened to, empathised with and understood. But doctors instinctively focus on other things – making a diagnosis, and prescribing treatment. In my experience, many doctors are not good listeners. Many do not empathise well with their patients.

The average consultation with a GP lasts between seven and fifteen minutes. When you subtract the time taken up by the doctor taking a medical history, carrying out physical examinations, doing and arranging tests, writing prescriptions and letters, informing the patient about the prescribed medications, arranging referrals, making and taking phone calls, writing in and going through the chart, patients will be lucky to get five minutes in which to express themselves to the doctor. Patients will be aware that the doctor does not have enough time to give them a full and proper hearing.

Rather than risk being cut short by the doctor, many people decide not to open up. They keep their pain to themselves. Without realising it, the doctor has confirmed their worst fears – that no one will listen to their story. Such an approach by a doctor or psychiatrist could be the last straw, reinforcing their belief that no one understands their pain. Thus the person's isolation and hopelessness is heightened – final confirmation that suicide is the only way to end the pain of living.

Many people who attempt suicide attend their general practitioners a few weeks prior to the attempt to end their life. Psychiatrists maintain that GPs are failing to diagnose and treat depression (with antidepressant drugs). But there are other possible reasons why the visit to the GP might not ease the distress these people were experiencing. For people who are considering suicide, the process of withdrawing from life and people begins a long time before that last visit to the GP. By the time of this final consultation, they have withdrawn within themselves in a desperate attempt to protect themselves from hurt and rejection. They are close to complete withdrawal from reaching out to anyone.

The visit to the GP may become the patient's last hope. In the eyes of the patient, this can quite literally be a life-or-death consultation. If the meeting goes very well, the patient leaves the surgery feeling heard and understood. They feel that this doctor really cares. The hope engendered by that consultation may well bring them back from the brink of suicide. But if the visit does not go well – in the eyes of the patient – the suicidal person may leave the surgery with their suicidal inclination reinforced. This person needs an unhurried consultation. Typically, they will get between seven and fifteen minutes – not nearly enough time for one so vulnerable.

They are aching to be understood. Instead they are diagnosed, probably as having depression, and prescribed antidepressant drugs. They may not want drugs. They want someone to listen. But the doctor may not really listen. He treats the 'underlying diagnosis' with drugs, or refers them to a psychiatrist who is even more expert at diagnosing than the GP. Once a person tells their GP that they are seriously suicidal, the GP's focus changes, as they then attempt to convince the person to admit themselves to a psychiatric hospital. The patient needs the doctor to be with them. Instead the doctor will talk at them, albeit with sympathy. They desperately need to connect with the doctor, but the doctor wants to treat the 'mental illness'. The consultation ends. The patient does not feel heard. Not feeling heard is a form of rejection. When this rejection comes from a doctor – the expert – the doctor has confirmed the patient's worst fears. There is no hope. They are beyond help. No one will ever listen.

Rejection always hurts. But when you are close to suicide, the pain of rejection is unbearable. The patient may not reach out to anyone again. The risk of suicide has been significantly raised by this visit to the doctor. More than tablets or a diagnosis, people who are depressed or close to suicide need a lifeline, a close trusting relationship with their doctor or therapist, a relationship which gives them hope. For a person in the throes of emotional turmoil, knowing that someone connects with them in their pain frequently gives them the will to hold on to their life. This understanding is a crucial part of the doctor-patient relationship. This was clearly not the sort of relationship Mary had with her psychiatrists. Speaking of how she planned her suicide, she said:

> If I'm going to do it, I'd better make sure I do it properly, otherwise they [the psychiatrists] will lock me up for good.

Rather than seeing them as the lifeline she desperately needed, Mary felt very threatened and intimidated by her psychiatrists, as do many people who find themselves attending psychiatrists. After years of contact with the mental health services, she speaks of psychiatrists as if they were more like enemies to be avoided than the caring professionals they are expected to be.

The interviewer asked Mary what had helped her to recover. Mary's reply speaks volumes. The single factor was a loving relationship which had given her a sense of safety and understanding in her life that had been missing for years, if indeed she had ever possessed it. She does not mention psychiatry as being a help in her recovery – quite the opposite. She points out the damage that psychiatry can do:

> A lot of the potential of psychiatric patients is completely lost and smothered by the concentration on their illness. There are a lot of immensely talented people whose talent is completely burnt up and wasted in psychiatric hospitals.

Doctors do tend to concentrate on the 'illnesses' they have decided these people have, rather than on the enormous potential that lies within each human being.

Mary has come a long way from that time of utter despair and hopelessness which drove her to jump into the river Corrib. No credit to psychiatry for her recovery. She found the strength within herself to move away from that place of terror and turmoil. She recovered through having her human needs met; through a loving relationship, companionship, sharing, safety, security, and having a place to paint her own colours and hang her own pictures.

When Barbara first attended me, she felt stigmatised by her previous doctor's approach to her depression. Five minutes into her first visit to her GP regarding her emotional distress, the doctor told her she was suffering from depression, which was caused by a biochemical abnormality. Being told that her depression was a mental illness caused by a biochemical imbalance in her brain offered Barbara no hope. She was extremely angry with the GP; so much so that I asked her to express her anger in writing:

> It is probably the patient's belief that they are mentally ill that actually contributes to suicide and the hopelessness and despair. Unless that mental illness label is removed, not only will medical intervention be ineffective, it will contribute to suicide. I would not be alive today if I did not have the absolute love, understanding and encouragement of one priceless friend. What kept me alive was his belief in me. He could explain to me what was happening – that was what I needed most. An explanation of what depression was, and facing up to and feeling the reality of my childhood. That pain almost killed me – in ways it would have been so much easier to die.
>
> Depressed people feel it is their time to die because they have lost themselves. We feel that we ourselves have died. There is no greater loss than that. So why can't the medical profession see that we are not mentally ill? We are very

hurt human beings. We have tried so hard to be human to other people in our lives. It is our humanness that is our greatest strength, and probably it is also what causes us so much pain. I think that my humanness is the last thing I have held on to. I still feel other people's sadness and pain and I try to help. When that humanness goes from me, I'll give up.

Barbara had experienced many painful losses in her life. Her depression made sense, given how her life had unfolded. Her life story was complex, as are all life stories. Yet her previous GP, who hardly knew her, presumed to know in five minutes that her depression was caused by a biochemical abnormality.

There is no public currency or language for depression. If you break a leg, your cast is obvious to everyone, evoking instant reactions of caring and understanding from family and strangers alike. Not so with depression or other 'mental illnesses'. The reactions from family, friends, strangers and workmates on hearing that someone is depressed can compound that person's isolation and loneliness.

Why Is the Risk of Suicide Greatly Increased Following Psychiatric Admission?

Research shows that there is a greatly increased risk that patients who have been discharged from psychiatric hospitals will take their own lives. Dr David Gunnell is a senior lecturer in epidemiology and public health medicine at the department of social medicine at Bristol

University. At the annual conference of the Irish Association of Suicidology in 1998 Dr Gunnell spoke about
groups with an increased risk of suicide.

According to Dr Gunnell, alcoholics, drug misusers,
Samaritan clients and people with a history of deliberate
self-harm are twenty times more likely to take their own
life than the general population. Suicide is ten times more
likely in current or ex-psychiatric patients than in the
general population. But one group is in a different league
in terms of their suicide risk; patients discharged from
psychiatric hospitals are ten to twenty times more likely
to kill themselves within four weeks of their discharge
from hospital than current or ex-psychiatric patients. In
other words, patients discharged from psychiatric hospitals are 100 to 200 times more likely to kill themselves
than the general population within four weeks of their
discharge.

These figures tally with those of Goldacre and Seagroatt, published in *The Lancet* of 31 July 1993. Theirs
was a large-scale British research project. The records of
14,240 people were assessed for twelve months after they
had been discharged following a psychiatric admission to
hospital. The researchers found that the suicide rate was
greatly increased for the whole twelve months during
which the study was conducted. But the risk was particularly high during the first twenty-eight days following
discharge from hospital:

Deaths with a coroner's verdict of suicide in the
first twenty-eight days after discharge were 213
times more common for male and 134 times

more common for female patients than would be expected during twenty-eight days in the general population.

What does it say about the effectiveness of psychiatric care when patients have a greatly increased risk of suicide after discharge from the psychiatric ward? Surely if psychiatric care were effective, patients would be less likely to take their life as a result of the treatment given while in hospital, not more so.

Diabetic patients do not leave hospital with an increased risk of going into a diabetic coma. If it were found that people admitted to hospital with an asthma attack were more likely to have another attack shortly after their discharge, there would be a public outcry.

In discharging a person from hospital, the psychiatrist is in effect stating that this person has improved to the point where he is no longer likely to take their own life. Perhaps psychiatrists do not know their patients well enough. When people spend seven to ten days in a psychiatric ward, they may have little contact with the consultant psychiatrist under whose care they were admitted to hospital. Rather than give the person time and safety to open up, the consultant typically concentrates on the diagnosis rather than on the person. The psychiatrist focuses on the (drug) treatment, rather than establishing a therapeutic and healing relationship between patient and doctor. Once the patient has been admitted, it is unusual for the psychiatrists to spend more than five or ten minutes a day with their patients. They feel they don't need to. The 'diagnosis' has been made, and 'treatment' commenced. The psychiatrist feels he has carried out his duties successfully in accordance with the job specifications.

But this is not good enough, and often patients and their families know that. The patient frequently leaves hospital feeling worse than when they were admitted, although they may not reveal this to their doctors. Patients know that if they say they are not getting better, they will be kept in hospital longer. They will probably be put on stronger medication than they are already on, with worse side effects. Worse still, they might be given ECT (shock therapy), against their will if necessary. Or the psychiatrists may insist they are signed into the mental institution against their will, removing from the patient the right to discharge themselves as a voluntary patient. So patients learn to lie to their psychiatrists to preserve their freedom. Many hospital patients learn how to play the game of 'becoming the good and obedient psychiatric patient'.

Goldacre and Seagroatt concluded:

> When an individual commits suicide after discharge from hospital, especially soon afterwards, the appropriateness of the discharge and the adequacy of supporting services in the community may be questioned.

The many psychiatrists involved in this study (and there were many, given how large this study was: 14,240 patients, who between them had a total of 26,864 psychiatric admissions in six different health districts) were apparently not very good at identifying people with high suicide intent.

Jim went through a difficult time when his marriage hit a rocky patch. Between us, we decided that Jim should be admitted to a psychiatric hospital for his own safety, since he had become preoccupied with taking his own life. However, the experience was so dreadful that he discharged himself after five days. Doctors and nurses asked him many questions, but they showed little willingness to listen to him. Jim desperately wanted someone to talk through his problems with him, but when he asked for counselling, he was told that it would not help him. The two medications prescribed for him made him feel strange. In five days, his consultant psychiatrist spoke with him for about ten minutes in total. Jim neither liked nor trusted this psychiatrist, who seemed more interested in figuring out what was 'wrong' with Jim than in relating to him.

Jim did learn something from his psychiatric admission. The shock of his experience in hospital catapulted him to a realisation that either he would work through his crisis without going into hospital or he would kill himself. Thankfully, he has come through his crisis. We continued to meet weekly, and sometimes twice-weekly for months after his discharge. In contrast, most psychiatric in-patients have little or no supportive follow-up after discharge. Jim was sure of one thing; come hell or high water he would never again be admitted to a psychiatric hospital. Thankfully, with counselling Jim has come to terms with his marital problems. But his hospital experience illustrates how the trauma of being a psychiatric in-patient can push you towards suicide, rather than pull you back from it.

YOUNG PEOPLE AND THE MEDICAL PROFESSION

There is disturbing evidence that young people do not see the medical profession as being approachable in a time of crisis. A 1998 study by Dr M. O'Sullivan and Professor M. Fitzgerald was published in the *Journal for the Association of Professionals in Services for Adolescents*. The study focused on teenage attitudes to suicide. The researchers found that only 15 per cent of those interviewed would recommend psychiatric help to someone who spoke about killing themselves. In another study carried out by the National Suicide Research Foundation in 1998, 100 university students were interviewed. Not one of these students mentioned GPs as a possible route to getting help if they were thinking of harming themselves or ending their life. According to this study, GPs are probably the last recourse for young people who are seriously depressed and considering suicide. The researchers concluded that: 'The youth don't see doctors as people they can turn to for help.'

A 1994 survey of the attitudes of teenagers to health and health care was carried out by Dr Jones, Dr Finlay, Dr Simpson and Tricia Kreitman BSc. The study was published in the *British Journal of General Practice* in October 1997. The survey revealed some alarming information concerning how teenagers view the general practice medical care system. Nine out of ten teenagers would prefer to visit a special teenage clinic than their own GP. More than nine out of ten did not want their own GP to run these clinics.

I have heard psychiatrists attributing this reluctance to attend the medical profession as a reflection of young people's inability to ask for help. While this may partly explain why young people do not seek medical help, there is another possible explanation which is less palatable to the medical profession. Maybe the reason young people are not reached by doctors is because they do not trust the medical healthcare system.

Perhaps teenagers believe that their pain and isolation will not be fully understood by doctors; that GP consultations rarely last more than fifteen minutes – not nearly enough time for them to express what they really need to say. Perhaps they feel that doctors are part of a powerful establishment which scares them; that doctors are far more likely to concentrate on prescribing a drug rather than hearing their deep anguish. They may dread that what they tell the GP will get back to their parents. And most frightening of all, if they tell the GP how badly they really feel, they may quickly end up in a psychiatric hospital, possibly against their will, labelled as 'mentally ill', with all the stigma and humiliation that go with a psychiatric hospital admission.

For the sake of our young people, the medical profession must face up to a painful truth. The medical service is being largely rejected by adolescents and young adults. 'Expert' views will make no impression on suicide rates if this critical issue is not addressed. It is time that modern medicine stopped telling people what is good for them and started listening to the views of ordinary people.

SUICIDE AND 'PSYCHIATRIC ILLNESS' – INFORMING THE PUBLIC
In *The Irish Times* of 27 March 2001, medical correspondent Dr Muiris Houston claimed that there is now a definite

biological explanation for suicide. Throughout his article, Dr Houston linked suicide to low levels of serotonin in the brain. Medical preoccupation with establishing a link between serotonin levels and suicide is not new. Until his death in 1998, Cork psychiatrist Dr Michael Kelleher was highly regarded within the British Isles as an expert on suicide. In an interview with John Waters in *The Irish Times* of 8 January 1991, Dr Kelleher expressed considerable enthusiasm for a link between low serotonin and suicide:

> There is now strong evidence that biochemical levels may be a strong factor in the new wave of young suicides. This research indicates that people with low levels of a substance called serotonin are more likely to commit suicide.

Four years later, however, Dr Kelleher's enthusiasm for a link between serotonin and suicide had apparently waned considerably. In the *Irish Medical Journal* of January/February 1995, an article was published that he co-wrote with Dr Fergus Shanahan, Professor of Medicine at University College Cork. Dr Kelleher wrote:

> Only a minority of suicide attempters show the relevant changes in serotonin metabolism. It is possible that the connection between suicide and serotonin has been overstretched.

Perhaps disillusioned with the lack of real progress in linking serotonin to suicide, in this article (entitled 'Psychoimmunology and Suicidal Behaviour') Dr Kelleher shifted his attention towards possible links between suicide and the immune system. Furthermore, in her 1997 book *A Guide to Psychiatry in Primary Care*, psychiatrist Patricia Casey cautioned that the serotonin–suicide link remained unproven:

> Recently there has been a growth of interest in the biology of suicide, and the role of serotonin in suicidal behaviour has been investigated, as has that of noradrenaline and dopamine. The results are as yet inconclusive.

In my opinion, the link between serotonin levels and suicide is far from established. To claim that there is now definite biological evidence for suicidal behaviour is, I believe, quite premature and potentially very confusing for the public who read such confident statements. Dr Houston's article was part of a major *Irish Times* investigation into suicide. Only one article of three days of reports articulated the views of people who had themselves made serious suicide attempts. This article, written by Pádraig ó Morain and published on 28 March 2001, presented the personal accounts of three people who had been deeply suicidal earlier in their lives. Ironically, since this three-day investigation predominantly highlighted the benefits of the medical approach to suicide, none of the three people reported that their recovery was as a result of medication, or the medical/psychiatric system. Rather, each attributed their recovery to sharing problems with others, friendship, receiving support and affirmation through support groups and learning to express their feelings and work through their problems.

One man whose story was featured said that he did not get better, despite psychiatric help. His recovery began when he became involved with GROW, a mental health support group which provided him with support and friendship.

> The enormous outpouring of welcome and the understanding and acceptance on these people's faces – that was really the first step on my journey to recovery.

A second man reported that he spent more than five weeks in a psychiatric hospital and more than six months 'on medication, going around like a zombie'. He said:

> I kept things to myself. You couldn't admit you weren't good, that was one of the biggest problems. Big boys don't cry. People need to talk about it. A trouble shared is a trouble halved. You realise then that other people have the same problem as yourself.

The third person who was featured in the article described her experience:

> I was put on medication which was to take over my life for seven years. I became totally addicted.

Reflecting the sense of hopelessness that many psychiatric patients pick up from their doctors, she said that 'nobody had told me in the six or seven years I had been going through the system that I could be well.' In the only part of the entire article which was in any way positive towards the psychiatric system, this woman's first admission to a psychiatric hospital seems to have helped her. But rather than attributing her improvement to psychiatric treatment, the biggest relief, she felt, was not having to hide her distress anymore:

> The secret was out. Everyone knew that I was sick, and for me that was the greatest relief of my life.

For these people, it seems that having their human needs met through human contact, support and understanding benefited them far more than medication for a hypothetical serotonin or other brain chemical imbalance. Are the medical experts hearing what their patients are telling them?

In my opinion, the lack of logical thought shared by many doctors regarding the cause of depression and other so-called 'psychiatric illnesses' revealed itself in the book *No One Saw My Pain* (1994) by psychiatrist Andrew Slaby. In his book, Dr Slaby takes an in-depth look at eight young people who attempted suicide, some of whom did not survive the attempt. While I am not doubting the author's compassion and sincerity, I believe that some of his conclusions lack common sense, being heavily influenced by traditional psychiatric beliefs and practices. He writes:

> Today [1994] depression is better understood than before. It is a biological vulnerability that

surfaces when sufficient disturbing life experiences occur.

The author shares with most of his psychiatrist colleagues the belief that depression is a biological disorder. He presents his belief to the general public as if it were an established fact – 'depression is a biological vulnerability'. But since there is no proof that the cause of depression is a biological defect, he is (albeit unintentionally) mis-informing the public. Yet the stories of these eight young people, as told by Dr Slaby, point to emotional, psych-ological, social and relationship problems within their lives, rather than a biological defect:

Were their cries not heard? No, something was heard: Chad's silence, Sarah's continuous crying, Carly's rage, Tim's reactions to an abusive father, Kent's mental illness, David's drug use, and John's anxiety about his sexuality.

The 'mental illness' which one of the eight young people (Kent) suffered from is stated to be schizophrenia. It is clear from the book that emotional distress and troubled relationships were central to Kent's so-called 'mental illness'. After Kent's suicide, his mother said:

I can never forgive Tom [Kent's father] for not meeting Kent's needs. But what can I say? I wasn't there for him either.

The author acknowledges that the enormous focus on depression within medicine is not having any effect on the suicide rate:

> Adolescent depression is recognised, diagnosed and treated more frequently than even five years ago. And yet the escalating statistics of adolescent suicide seem to nullify any serious progress.

Dr Slaby's book was published in 1994. In the intervening years, the medical profession has put enormous energy and publicity into diagnosing and treating depression, yet the suicide rate continues to escalate. As a traditional psychiatrist, Dr Slaby believes that antidepressant medication is central to recovery from depression. He states that depression is a very treatable illness. Here we have a paradox which repeatedly shows itself in psychiatry. If depression is now recognised, diagnosed and better treated, and if depression is the most common cause of suicide, why is the suicide rate rising dramatically?

When something is repeated often enough, it becomes widely accepted as gospel truth. Modern medicine's repeated assertion that the cause of depression is bio-chemical has become widely accepted as a fact. In *The Teenage Years,* which was jointly written by broadcaster Fergal Keane and psychologist M. Murray, the authors discuss the causes of depression in the traditional psychiatric fashion: two main groups, reactive and endogenous. Reactive depression is described as depression for which there is an understandable cause. It is their comment on the second group – endogenous depression – that caught my eye:

> Endogenous/biological depression: This form of
> depression normally has more biological origins
> and less immediate environmental triggers. As
> a result, there is often no discernible or
> apparent cause.

This statement is factually incorrect and therefore mis-leading, albeit unwittingly. This book is written for the general public, who cannot be expected to have a deep understanding of mental health. When the authors make a statement which implies that what is said is a known fact, the general public will accept it as such. When they write that 'this form of depression normally has more biological origins and less environmental triggers', the public will naturally accept this on face value. But no proof exists that the cause of *any* form of depression is biological in origin.

The authors' use of the term 'endogenous/biological depression' is most unfortunate. It implies that endogenous and biological are interchangeable terms, compounding the misinformation. They are not interchangeable because it has not been established that depression has a biological cause. Medicine is filled with elitist words, a language which mystifies the subject and prevents the public from under-standing medical terminology. Endogenous depression is an elitist term. To the man in the street, this title sounds impressive. But the real meaning of the term 'endogenous depression' is that 'we doctors don't know what is causing this so we assume it originates within the person'. Doctors frequently label people as suffering from endogenous depression because many doctors are not skilled enough to identify subtle triggers for the depression, triggers which may go back to the person's childhood.

Other examples of medical misinformation on depression, 'mental illness' and suicide are commonplace in the media. It is understandable that journalists take what the medical experts claim with such authority to be established fact. For example, Christopher Russell wrote in the *Sunday Independent* of 13 September 1998:

> The fact is that up to 90 per cent of suicide deaths are linked with some form of psychiatric illness (usually depression). Endogenous depression is primarily a biological complaint caused by an imbalance in the brain. It is frequently hereditary.

Here is another example of medical theories being presented to the public as if they are established facts. Three statements are here stated as fact when in truth they are merely theories. It is not a fact that 90 per cent of suicides are due to psychiatric illness. Nor is it true to say that endogenous depression is a biological complaint. And there is no solid evidence that depression is hereditary. While depression is more common in families where parents are depressed, this might just as well be due to the emotional effect of a depressed parent on children.

ANTIDEPRESSANTS AND SUICIDE

Most doctors (and consequently the public) believe that antidepressant drugs are very successful at treating depression. And since depression is the major cause of suicide, doctors also believe that antidepressants prevent suicide, one might reasonably expect that antidepressant treatment is known to be effective in reducing the suicide rate.

No such evidence exists. According to psychiatrist Dr J. F. Connolly in the *Irish Medical News* of 7 September 1998:

> For many years, in spite of the fact that antidepressants were widely available and widely prescribed, it did not appear that they had any effect on the suicide rates for depressed patients.

Antidepressants have become more and more frequently prescribed during the past twenty-five years. One in twelve women and one in twenty-eight men in Britain are currently on antidepressants, but the suicide rate keeps rising. When doctors speak in public on the prevention of suicide through antidepressant drugs, they do not inform the public that this is an unproven hypothesis. They usually convey the impression that this has already been established.

According to *Suicide in Ireland: A Global Perspective and a National Strategy,* the 1998 Aware report on suicide, there is evidence that antidepressant drugs may actually increase the risk of suicide:

> A review conceded that the effectiveness of individual psychiatric and psychotherapeutic treatment remains unproven for suicide

prevention. There is some suggestion that maintenance treatment with antidepressant drugs to prevent recurrences of depression may increase the suicide rate. This risk is considered to be small, but it points to the fact that long-term antidepressant use may precipitate a cycling instability of mood, while still having an antidepressant effect.

In my opinion, this is an example of how – perhaps without realising it – doctors come up with explanations which do not undermine their own beliefs or their treatments. I believe that to say that antidepressants produce mood instability while still working as effective antidepressants is contradictory. If the antidepressants were working, patients would not have these unstable mood swings. But the experts need some way of explaining this without undermining the 'effectiveness' of their treatments.

8

PREVENTING SUICIDE

In the British Isles there is a concerted drive to treat depression with antidepressant drugs. The experts (psychiatrists mainly) explain why: psychiatry has 'established' that those who take their lives are 'psychiatrically ill'. The most commonly found illness is depression. Therefore, if we blitz the nation, searching for cases of depression and treat them, the suicide rate should be reduced dramatically. A major driving force behind this national blitz is the pharmaceutical industry, which stands to make millions from this approach. These medical experts really come across as if they know they are doing the right thing, and I do not doubt that they believe they are doing the right thing.

PREVENTION POLICIES BASED ON PRESUMPTION

Dr D. J. Gunnell is a senior British lecturer in public health. He does not appear convinced that the current health strategy on suicide is known to be effective. In 1998, in his presentation to the national conference of the Irish Association of Suicidology, he said that the effectiveness of health service efforts to prevent suicide is based on speculation:

> GP education programmes, and antidepressant and lithium prescribing require further investigation, as does the role played by telephone counselling services (such as the Samaritans).

Dr Gunnell makes a valid point. The effectiveness of psychiatry's attempts to reduce suicide *are* unproven, but that is not how psychiatry portrays the situation to the general public. Through the media, psychiatrists repeatedly inform the public that effective drug treatments are now available for depression, and that by treating depression we will reduce the suicide rate. They do not say that their approach is speculative.

UNDERSTANDING SUICIDAL BEHAVIOUR IS NOT ENOUGH

The phrase 'suicidal behaviour' is quite popular within modern medicine. Medical experts repeatedly emphasise that in order to reduce the suicide rate, doctors must develop a better understanding of suicidal behaviour. I do not believe that in general psychiatry has a deep understanding of the human condition. I do not see how doctors can develop a thorough understanding of suicidal behaviour unless they adopt a much broader approach to people in emotional crisis.

Suicidal behaviour cannot be understood without looking at the deeper issues. The reason why modern medicine is not getting anywhere on the suicide issue can be traced back to how the medical profession sees a human being. Doctors are trained to look almost exclusively at the physical aspect of people – the human body and how the various organs and systems in the body function and interact with each other. Most doctors know little about other aspects of the human being, such as the emotional and psychological aspects of human existence. Doctors focus on suicidal behaviour as if suicide can be tackled by understanding this behaviour. But it cannot. Behaviour of any sort will only be understood when:

- The feelings which prompted the behaviour are understood – feelings of worthlessness, hopelessness, deep insecurity and vulnerability
- The emotional needs which the person is trying to meet through their behaviour are recognised and understood. Suicide is one way of ensuring that there will be no more rejection and abandonment. Suicide is the ultimate act of avoidance when the pain of living has become too overwhelming. Suicidal behaviour is often a cry for help. Because of the distressed state of the person, the signs may be subtle and go unnoticed. On the other hand, the cry for help may be heard and acted upon. Emotionally vulnerable people rarely feel safe enough to ask for the real help they need. They will rarely say 'I feel deeply distressed and emotionally vulnerable; I cannot cope any more, please help me', especially if they are men. Through suicidal behaviour they may drop hints to those around them that they really need help. But the clues may be heavily disguised. By disguising the cries for help the emotion-

ally vulnerable person protects themselves from further hurt and rejection they might experience by exposing their deep vulnerability and not receiving the support, love and acceptance for which they crave.

If we are to understand and prevent suicide, we need to see suicide and suicidal behaviour as it truly is: a protective act of avoidance. It is protective because by ending their life, the person guarantees that their pain, their deep emotional vulnerability, their isolation, loneliness, and desperate fear of rejection and abandonment are over – forever. Suicide also puts an end to the pain of self-rejection, a constant torment for people in emotional turmoil.

THE THERAPIST

What sort of therapist works most effectively with people who are emotionally distressed? A GP? A psychiatrist? A psychologist? A psychotherapist? A counsellor? A friend? GPs do not give people enough time to express themselves or to explore the issues which are at the root of the problem. Nor do they currently have enough understanding of the human emotions and behaviour to make a meaningful and effective contribution. GPs are pre-occupied with diagnosing so-called 'psychiatric illness'. Once there is any trace of depression or any 'mental illness', the prescription pad comes into play and the real listening stops. I believe that both GPs and psychiatrists prescribe antidepressant drugs and tranquillizers far too often and far too easily.

I do not believe that psychiatry in its present form should be the foundation stone upon which effective therapy is built. Through its close relationship with the pharmaceutical industry, psychiatry has tied itself to a future where only selective medical research will be carried out.

Psychiatry is prepared to explore one form of 'talk' therapy' – cognitive-behavioural therapy, in which therapists attempt to create more positive patterns of thinking and behaving within the person. While this form of therapy may well work for some people, in my opinion psychotherapy needs a broader, more comprehensive approach than that of cognitive-behavioural therapy. The thought has struck me that one reason for psychiatry's acceptance of cognitive-behavioural therapy as opposed to other forms of psychotherapy might be that cognitive-behavioural therapy represents no threat to psychiatry. It can easily be brought into the medical model alongside drug treatments. While more comprehensive psychotherapy can – and sometimes should – also be used alongside medication, these therapies sometimes disagree with the medical profession's extensive use of medication for emotional problems. Therefore psychotherapy in general represents a threat to psychiatry's dominant position in the treatment of 'mental illness'. Perhaps it is no wonder that most psychiatrists show little enthusiasm for psychotherapy.

A common misconception is that psychotherapy is still based on Sigmund Freud's approach. Increasingly over the past fifty years, Freud's views have diminished in importance. While many approaches to psychotherapy retain a varying proportion of his ideas, to describe psychotherapy flippantly as 'Freud's talk therapy' – as I have heard psychiatrists and journalists do – is to display one's own ignorance of the enormous changes which have occurred within psychotherapy in the past fifty years.

I believe that in the majority of psychiatric research, the cart has been put before the horse. The outcome – that emotional and psychological problems are 'illnesses' caused by brain chemical imbalances or genetic defects – is presumed long before it has been established. Consequently, I believe that psychiatry's role in health care needs to be reformed significantly. But the momentum of modern psychiatry towards the 'mental illness' approach has gathered such pace that reform may be greatly resisted by mainstream psychiatry.

I believe that the kind of therapists we need are more likely to come from the realm of psychology, psychotherapy and counselling rather than from the medical profession. Therapists must give people enough time to express themselves. They must have a deep understanding of what it means to be human. They need to be compassionate people who are balanced enough to show great caring and concern for their clients yet not become sucked into the person's problems. They must respect and care for their clients as equal human beings, not as inferior or less knowledgeable people than the therapists themselves. They must be superb listeners who know how to raise people's self-esteem. They must know how to create a safe, therapeutic relationship with their clients.

Therapists need to be prepared to meet with their clients in their despair and pain. They should seek to help people solve their own issues rather than jump in with their own solutions. It is not always so much a question of how much the doctor or therapist knows. It is human

understanding and compassion, and how well he com-
municates this caring that matters. If therapists lose sight
of these fundamental qualities, they can do their clients
more harm than good. While there are many therapists
who work to these standards, the counselling professions
still have some way to go.

There are many schools of therapy promoting different
approaches. Some therapists believe they must tell the client
what to do. Others believe therapy should be non-directive
– the therapist deliberately resists the temptation to tell
clients what is best for them. Studies have shown that the
most important factor in successful therapy is not what type
of therapy is used; the important factors are the quality of
the relationship between client and therapist and the
commitment of the client. One reason why the counselling
professions have failed to break psychiatry's stronghold on
so-called 'mental illness' is their lack of a unified and
coordinated approach to counselling. This makes it much
easier for psychiatry to divide and conquer the counselling
professions. But perhaps the willingness of counselling and
psychotherapy to countenance different approaches is
healthier than psychiatry's more tunnel-visioned approach.

THE VIEWS OF AN EXPERIENCED COUNSELLOR

Jim Byrne is a senior counsellor at University College,
Galway, who has been counselling students for many
years. I am very grateful for his contribution, in which he
outlines his own beliefs about the current suicide prevention policy, its limitations, and his views on how to
help people who feel suicidal:

Suicide is a very complex phenomenon, and in many cases, the suicidal mind is not a sick mind. Social isolation, family disharmony, unemployment, relationships and other personal issues are commonly found in the treatment of those who are suicidal. These issues are rarely addressed when these people are admitted to the psychiatric services. However, what is even more important is that the psychological terrain of the mind of the would-be suicidal victim is often not even looked at. Unendurable psychological pain, feelings of helplessness and hopelessness, isolation and despair are always present in the lives of those who wish to end their lives. No one commits suicide out of joy; the enemy of their life is pain. Pain is what the person committing suicide seeks to escape.

Suicide is not random. It is never done pointlessly or without purpose. Suicide is both a movement away from pain and a movement to end consciousness. This area, the emotional and psychological pain, must become the major focus in the management of suicide. These issues demand that skilled professionals and caring individuals be given the opportunity to work with those at risk. The incidence of suicide can be lowered and many young lives saved if those in daily contact with the individual can learn to recognise and intervene effectively when they hear that all-important cry for help. Not all cries for help receive the attention they need. Commitment to a psychiatric unit or a mandatory psychiatric interview while in hospital recovering from the suicide attempt will not suffice. If we, the professionals, don't address these early warning signs professionally, how can we expect society to do so?

In my own experience of counselling those at risk of suicide at university, I have very rarely found the need to involve the local psychiatric services. Most young people who are suffering from emotional or social problems are greatly relieved when they find someone who listens to them and who can identify with the mental anguish they are feeling at the time. Also, to have someone who will intervene in the areas that are causing them to be suicidal is a major factor in enabling them to look at the future, less burdened and more hopeful.

I have found over the past twenty years of counselling that if these inner psychological issues and needs are addressed in counselling, it is rare that suicide will occur. This form of management of those at risk of suicide is not the model used in the present-day psychiatric services. This is not a reflection on these services but, as they depend on a medical/ chemical solution to solve the emotional pain of those at risk, they have very little to offer. The psychiatric model of treatment does not address these important areas of the individual sufferer's life, and until our health services train and sensitise relevant professional staff to work in these areas, it is my opinion that our suicide rates will not be reduced.

The views of Jim Byrne and others whose views differ somewhat from the approach of modern medicine need to be afforded the same attention as those of modern medicine itself. The prevailing view of the medical profession should no longer be accepted at face value. The time has come to find out what an expert really means when he says 'We now know that. . . '. Far too often, it would be more correct for the expert to say 'we now *believe* that. . . '. We must put an end to the practice of presenting theories as if they were established facts. We must bring together the best brains we have, the people with the deepest understanding of the human condition.

We must listen to leading and experienced psychologists, psychotherapists and counsellors much more than we have done in the past. We cannot allow modern medicine to monopolise the 'expert' position any longer. We must get beyond the presumption that people end their lives because they have a 'psychiatric illness'. We need to look at the real issues behind suicide – low self-esteem, human vulnerability, relationship conflicts, emotional, social, psychological and life issues.

SELF-BELIEF COMES WHEN SOMEONE BELIEVES IN YOU

In the following case history, Annette touches on some important issues which emerge again and again in the care of emotionally distressed people: the 'antidepressant-at-the-drop-of-a-hat' mentality of the medical profession;

the side effects of antidepressants, including the alarming and unnatural highs which Annette experienced and the lows she felt when the drug was stopped; the process of withdrawal from life which people who are emotionally vulnerable go through but which is interpreted by doctors as a sign of 'mental illness'.

Annette's admission to a psychiatric ward which was supposed to help her turned out to be the most traumatic experience of her life. Many of the doctors she encountered before me failed to establish a trusting and compassionate relationship with her. The quality of her relationship with me became the springboard for her recovery. It is clear from her writing that she needed people to believe in her, to really listen to her. To see her potential, even if she could not see it herself:

I am a professional woman in my twenties. Almost a year ago, I was at my lowest ebb. My self-esteem was minuscule and my self-doubting huge. My self-confidence was so non-existent that I beat myself up internally for everything I did. Life became so bleak that I could never envisage the dim light at the end of an endless tunnel drawing near. It is hard to describe the awful empty feelings of unworthiness and self-hate that crept up on me very slowly and unconsciously. Bit by bit I began to withdraw from routine daily tasks, until I reached the point where life had no meaning.

I could not see any point in getting up in the morning. I would set my alarm at night, begging myself to wake up in the morning. But every morning I would inevitably reach out and switch off the alarm. Staying in bed became yet another reason to hate myself – I now had laziness to add to my long list of faults. I stayed in bed until late in the afternoon. If visitors called to our house, I would shy away and hide until they left. Enjoyable events like going out socialising or even going into town shopping became huge undertakings. I became totally obsessed with what other people thought of me, both physically and of my personality. I felt that total strangers were looking distastefully at me, and this made me withdraw even more.

My friends were unaware of these changes. I always covered up how I felt, making conversations with friends centre around them rather than around me and my life. I threw in the odd white lie about how I was and what I was doing, which led to more lies, and guilt for good measure. I bottled up all my problems and worries because I was afraid I would lose my friends if they knew the real me – problems, flaws, warts and all. It all became a vicious circle, trying to remember what I had told different people, trying to keep up the pretence. Looking back now, I was always a sensitive child and I developed coping strategies at an early age. When I left college and had the responsibility of work and the real world, stress really became a problem for me.

I was very unhappy in my job. My social life was hectic – I didn't have one free night in the week. Then my father got very sick and was in hospital for several months. His illness greatly increased the stress within all our family, including myself. One day I broke down and told one friend how unhappy I really was. I couldn't stop sobbing. On my friend's advice, I attended both a GP and a psychologist. The GP started me on medication for depression, and the psychologist tried to raise my self-esteem. For a few months I felt a bit better, but then I became so depressed I was unable to work. The GP's advice was to go back on the anti-depressants again for a minimum of three months. Reluctantly, I took the medication, as I was determined to fight these blues for once and for all. I didn't improve, and my GP referred me to a psychiatrist. I had major side effects from all the medication the psychiatrist prescribed. Eventually the psychiatrist put me back on the medication my GP had prescribed. I took the drugs, this time for four months, coming off them gradually.

Four months later I again became depressed, but this time it was much deeper. I went to my GP again and the same medication was prescribed. After two months, I became very high-spirited and loud on the medication. My friend could see that all was not well and arranged for me to see a different psychiatrist.

This doctor said that I was too high and that I should come off this antidepressant. He offered additional medication – which I didn't take – to ease the transition off these tablets. Having had so many problems with antidepressant drugs, I did not feel like being a guinea-pig again. Three days after stopping the antidepressants I felt very low. I became very frightened, so I asked to be admitted to hospital – I felt I would be safer there.

I was admitted to a psychiatric hospital for three weeks – one of the best known and most highly regarded psychiatric hospitals in the country. This was the most traumatic experience I have ever had in my life. The staff were incredibly condescending and patronising in the beginning. All sharp objects – like scissors, tweezers, razors were taken from me. The nurses combed through my bags in case I was hiding some implement with which I could injure myself. My own word didn't mean anything, everything had to be double-checked. I was fully locked in initially but after four days I was moved to a different ward where I had more freedom. Some of the other patients really frightened me. I felt very uncomfortable also because one of the male patients had a crush on me and kept following me around and giving me tapes of love songs.

After three weeks I was discharged with a psychological assessment which stated that I had 'low self-esteem'. I still did not feel any better and the psychiatrists had nothing else to offer me. I could not get an appointment with my psychologist for three months. I went to see a different counsellor, who advised me to take time out from work to sit with my feelings. But when I wasn't working I had nothing to do. I was also conscious of preserving my financial independence. I was afraid that if I was not working, my neighbours would say that I was different. And I was scared. I retreated into myself more and more.

Eventually I could not even go to church in case I'd meet anyone. I visited my psychologist, who kept insisting that I go to my GP for medication to speed up my recovery. I was adamant that I would never again put another psychiatric tablet into my mouth. We argued and disagreed on that point. I was getting nowhere with the psychologist. He kept telling me that what I needed to do was to change my whole way of thinking from negative to positive, but I found this impossible to do. If you are feeling really low and self-critical, you can't change your way of thinking like flicking on a switch. It didn't work for me anyhow. I felt that because I wasn't getting better, the psychologist became frustrated with me, and we seemed to argue for most of our meetings.

My friend heard about Dr Terry Lynch and I made an appointment with him. I was so pleased with my first visit, I was sure my second visit couldn't be as good, but it was. He listened attentively and accepted me as the person I am. He totally understood my dilemma. I sensed that he was genuinely concerned and compassionate. He explained everything clearly. His message was clear: that in his opinion, I did not have a mental illness. He felt that I was emotionally low and as a result my self-confidence was also low. He assured me that my negative thinking was perfectly natural as a defence mechanism due to the traumatic events in my life up to then. His positive and understanding outlook was uplifting.

It was obvious that he had been listening to me very carefully. Through his genuine belief and confidence in my ability I began to feel important. He didn't push me to do anything I didn't feel ready for. After our third meeting, I was back doing certain tasks I had been avoiding. I tentatively went back to part-time work and I kept in telephone contact with Terry every few days for encouragement and support. His genuine interest in me gave me enough belief in myself to begin socialising again for the first time in well over a year. I began to apply for better jobs, and to my amazement, I got called for several interviews. I actually got job offers I didn't expect, which really boosted my confidence. During this time I kept in close contact with Terry, who kept reassuring me about my potential. His belief in me was a great help.

I feel in control of my life for the first time ever. I feel really empowered. I realise that I have a long way to go, but life is much more meaningful. It is important to evaluate one's achievements, to feel proud of having the courage to live again and thrilled with progress made. So many people give advice and judge us. It is so good to meet somebody who is a good listener and who is non-judgemental. I'm proof that anything is possible with the proper guidance and direction. Self-belief comes when other people believe in you.

Nelson Mandela once said that it is not our weakness that scares us, but our power. Some people feel so unsafe that they cannot believe in themselves, even when others do. To believe in oneself means taking action. If the action which needs to be taken is too overwhelming, the person may not be ready to develop their self-belief until they are at a safer place within themselves.

Annette recently rang me with the news that she had got a permanent job in a lovely location. Because she no longer feels the need to avoid people and lie about what she is doing, she now has a better social life. My belief in her helped her believe in herself. As her self-belief grew, Annette gradually reintegrated with the world at her own pace.

A Story of Hope

When I first met Jean, she was overcome with anxiety. As she entered my surgery, she was shaking uncontrollably, unable to put a sentence together. I had to get Jean's history from her sister, who accompanied her. Then thirty years old, Jean had been dominated by anxiety since she was a child. In the three months before attending me, Jean's anxiety had become extremely severe, despite her taking five tranquillizers and two sleeping tablets every day on medical advice. She had become increasingly withdrawn and had stayed indoors at home for weeks. She had virtually stopped eating and was not sleeping, in spite of all the medication. I had not seen a more severe case of anxiety in my fifteen years working as a doctor. Jean was having a nervous breakdown right in front of me. As it turned out, this was the beginning of a breakthrough for Jean, the beginning of her healing journey.

I was not sure how I should deal with this severely agitated person whom I had never met before. Five years previously I would have done the medically appropriate thing. I would have considered giving Jean an injection of a strong sedative. I would have carefully thought about admitting her to a psychiatric hospital, against her will if necessary. Five years previously, I would have known no other way.

I quickly realised that sending Jean to a psychiatric hospital was about the worst thing I could do for her. She was already consumed with terror; the emotional trauma that a psychiatric admission would create for Jean might be unbearable for her. I asked Jean to lie on my couch. She was rigid as a board, wide-eyed with panic, and continued to shake uncontrollably. I gently placed one hand on her stomach and one on her heart. I asked Jean to close her eyes and listen to my words. For thirty minutes, I quietly reassured her that she was safe now, that there was no threat to her.

Within five minutes, Jean stopped shaking. After thirty minutes, her eyes remained closed. She lay peacefully on the couch, as if in a deep, peaceful sleep. Jean's sister Helen remained in the room throughout. Watching Jean change from a state of severe panic to one of peace moved Helen deeply. Jean had relaxed so much that her limbs felt heavy and she was yawning. She could at last talk to me coherently. We arranged an appointment for a few days later. I did not prescribe any medication. I did not refer her to a psychiatrist. I could see that a central part of Jean's anxiety was that she felt very unsafe, threatened by the slightest thing. I felt that I could play a central role in her recovery by fostering a trusting and safe relationship with her over the coming months.

In the eighteen months since our first meeting, Jean has attended me about every fourteen days. She is making steady progress. As I had hoped, her relationship with me is a great source of safety and security for her. She eagerly looks forward to our meetings. Our relationship is built on respect and caring; she feels highly valued as an important and unique human being. As our relationship developed, Jean shared her life story with me. Before long, I could clearly see how her severe anxiety had developed. Her mother died suddenly when she was six. Jean was the youngest of a large family. Her family felt that she should be protected as much as possible from the pain of her mother's illness and death so Jean was not brought to visit her mother in hospital. When her mother died, Jean was kept away from the funeral. When she asked her family why her mummy was not at home any more, she received vague replies which further increased her confusion. It is important to say that at all times her family had her best interests at heart.

Within months of her mother's death, Jean became very anxious. She refused to go to school. She missed at least half of the following six school years. At thirteen years of age, she gave up school completely and got a job in a launderette. Four years later, she gave that up and she has not worked since. Over the past twelve years, Jean had become a recluse. She avoided all contact with people, only venturing out occasionally. She has never had a close relationship, or even a close friend. For ten years, Jean had been attending her local psychiatric hospital once a fortnight. The psychiatric doctors she attended moved on every six months to be replaced by a new batch. No sooner had she developed any degree of rapport with them then they disappeared from her life. Eventually she learned that there was little point in opening up to these doctors, since they would soon be moving on. She told me that her consultations with these doctors lasted no more than a few minutes. They concentrated on reviewing her notes and assessing her medication.

I asked her whether her years attending the psychiatrists had helped her. The only positive comment she made was about the relaxation classes, which initially helped her a little, but the effect was not lasting. She did not feel that the psychiatrists had been much help to her. Three months before we met, she stopped attending the psychiatric hospital. After ten years of frequent attendances, she was still taking five tranquillizers and two sleeping tablets a day, and getting nowhere.

The psychiatrists did not seem to know what to do next. Jean saw no hope in what they had to offer so she stopped attending. She became a total recluse, rarely venturing out even to the local shop. She spent most of her time in bed at home. Jean eventually reached a state of constant severe panic, as she was when she first attended me.

After eighteen months of working together, Jean, her sister and I all feel that she has made dramatic progress. She is sleeping better and her appetite has returned. Both the frequency and the severity of her anxiety is now a fraction of what it used to be eighteen months ago. She goes out and about at will every day. Without pressure from me, she has gradually reduced her tranquillizers. After years of taking seven tablets a day and still experiencing severe, ever-present anxiety, for the past five months she has not taken a single tablet. Jean's sister has told me that the family are amazed at Jean's improvement.

Psychiatry's approach to anxiety is quite simplistic. Anxiety is a 'disorder' which psychiatrists and doctors in general try to eliminate, usually with tranquillizers. In the eyes of psychiatry, anxiety is an illness per se, requiring medical treatment. Psychiatrists interpret people's problems according to their beliefs about 'mental illness'.

I do not believe that anxiety is an illness or a disorder. Anxiety is a natural human response to a situation which is perceived by the person as threatening to their safety, their security. Anxiety does not suddenly appear without reason like a bolt from the blue to be eliminated with tranquillizers or antidepressants. Anxiety is a protective reaction when life becomes very threatening. Severe anxiety is an unpleasant experience and people understandably attend doctors in order to seek relief. But the cause of the anxiety is often that the person's sense of safety and security is threatened. If the person is helped to address the safety and security issues in their lives, the anxiety will often spontaneously diminish.

The psychiatrists misinterpreted Jean's problem. They diagnosed Jean as having a severe anxiety disorder of unknown origin. In more than ten years, they did not focus on her vulnerability, her lack of inner safety and security. The seeds of Jean's anxiety problem were sown at six years of age, when her mother died. Every child builds their sense of safety and security around their parents. The psychiatrists treated the anxiety, as if the anxiety were the problem. Had they focused on the real issue – her total lack of any inner safety and security – they might have got somewhere. Jean's anxiety was not her problem – quite the opposite: it was her protector. Feeling constantly unsafe and under threat, her anxiety protected Jean from taking risks which would have left her open to further hurt. Even simple everyday things like going for a walk had become very threatening to her. While becoming a recluse was painful, it was less painful than taking any risks.

As a child, Jean had been very attached to her mother. Suddenly her mother was no longer there for her. Jean's safety net disappeared from her life. Her family's well-meaning decision not to discuss her mother's death with Jean unwittingly compounded the situation. Jean could not begin to understand what had happened. She was not given an explanation which made any sense to her. Jean's whole world was threatened. Her sense of safety and security in her life was pulled from under her.

Within weeks of her mother's death, Jean began to withdraw from life. She saw school as a highly threatening experience where she felt very vulnerable. Jean avoided school rather than endure extreme terror every day. Her response to life increasingly became one of avoidance and withdrawal. Jean's father drank heavily and was often aggressive at home. Jean did not have a close relationship with her father. Throughout her childhood, she had no one to turn to.

Now, for the first time in her life, she has a relationship with a doctor who she feels understands her. Every time I see her, I reassure her that there is nothing psychiatrically wrong with her. She now understands that her anxiety is the direct result of the immense lack of inner safety she has felt for years. She knows that the main thing I focus on in her sessions with me is for her to experience a deep sense of safety. A person can relax only when they feel safe, which is why the relaxation classes at the psychiatric hospital only gave her slight and temporary relief.

I did not concentrate on a diagnosis with Jean. I saw her as a normal healthy human being who had a major lack of safety in her life due to past events. I always concentrate on people's normality. Psychiatry always gave her the impression that she was abnormal. The psychiatrists she had attended for years gave her about five or seven minutes per consultation. Take from this the time it took to review her charts and write her prescription –

that left less than five minutes for interaction between Jean and the psychiatrist. No meaningful interaction can take place in five minutes. It is hardly surprising that Jean left those consultations with her loneliness and hopelessness increased.

Her consultations with me last an hour. I let Jean decide what direction she wanted our sessions to take. She gets immense safety and relaxation from our talks and relaxation sessions. I repeatedly emphasise to her that she is a unique and priceless human being. She knows that I hold her in high esteem and – unlike the psychiatric personnel, who moved on every six months – she knows that I will be here for her next week, next month, and in three years' time if needs be. She therefore has a great sense of safety, support and equality in her relationship with me. These qualities are vital in the healing process, but they were absent from her relationship with the psychiatrists she attended.

For the first time in years, Jean has a sense of hope for the future. I'm not pushing Jean to do anything. To do so would be to threaten her, to undermine her now growing sense of safety. I have not recommended that she force herself to do anything she's not ready for.

As we work together, Jean is coming out of her shell. Given the degree of hopelessness she felt prior to attending me, I believe that Jean might have chosen to take her own life but for the hope, trust and compassion she has experienced in her relationship with me. Jean dreaded going to see the psychiatrists. Because she felt so threatened by the psychiatrists, her anxiety always increased when she attended them. The symptoms the psychiatrists were trying to eradicate was actually being increased by those consultations. It is hardly surprising that their treatments did not work.

An analogy may help to illustrate what it's like to live in a constant state of anxiety. When a hurricane is approaching, people sit up and take notice. They barricade their windows, doors, businesses. If people have enough warning, they will spend twenty-four to forty-eight hours preparing for the hurricane, protecting themselves, their loved ones and their property. As the hurricane arrives, everyone withdraws into a place of safety until the storm has blown over. There is hardly a soul on the streets. Our TV screens regularly show us how hurricane-prone places such as Florida prepare for an oncoming hurricane. We all agree that this is a 'normal' human response. The hurricane is a major threat which requires a correspondingly major response from people living in the path of the hurricane.

For people whose anxiety is intense, like Jean, life is like one big terrifying hurricane, from which they constantly feel the need to withdraw to protect themselves from emotional annihilation. The same is true for emotionally distressed and vulnerable people who become depressed, or are diagnosed as schizophrenic. They feel as if every day is a huge threat to their very survival, filled with the risk of further rejection and emotional pain. So, understandably, they withdraw and put up the barricades, closing themselves off from people and from life.

I am currently working with many people with anxiety who attended psychiatrists and were treated with high doses of tranquillizers. Many of these people went to the psychiatrist with one problem and ended up with two: their anxiety, either not improved or heightened, and an addiction to tranquillizers – the 'treatment' prescribed by the experts.

RELATIONSHIPS AND THE FAMILY REVISITED

Few things in life are as important to people as relationships. No man is an island. The relationships children develop within their families are the foundations of so many critically important factors which have a huge bearing on the rest of their lives, including self-esteem, inner safety and security. Yet there is no mechanism in society to help people understand and improve how they relate to others. Relationship issues and difficulties are the real reason why many people attend doctors. But the relationship issue is rarely touched upon, let alone resolved. Consequently, thousands of people every year leave the doctor's surgery with a diagnosis which is misguided and a prescription they do not need, usually for either an antidepressant or a tranquillizer.

When there is a great human need, society has an obligation to do whatever is necessary to meet that need. People need protection, so society has created the defence forces and the legal system. People need health care: most countries responded to this need by creating a system of health care which is widely available to all. People need to put bread on the table. Social welfare systems have been developed as a response to this need.

The time has come for society to respond to the massive human need for emotional safety and security. The widespread occurrence of emotional distress, 'mental illness' and the tragedy of suicide is calling to us to put into place a system in society where people can get help to overcome relationship and life issues. The key importance of relationships and their immense influence on people's lives must receive appropriate recognition. A system should be devised which offers people help and understanding, to help them overcome problems created by relationships without judgement or blame.

These measures must be undertaken in a spirit of compassion for all concerned. Parents do their best for their children, but frequently parents' own need to protect themselves from further stress and hurt reduces their ability to provide their children with the greatest protection there is from 'mental' illnesses and suicide – high self-esteem, created by unconditionally loving relationships and open communication.

Critically important though they are, these issues are rarely discussed. They are brushed under the carpet. Yet those within troubled families often know the reality of the situation, that all is not well within the family. Fear of criticism and judgement prevents the parents in many such families from seeking help. Yet if help were available to parents in emotional difficulty, help based on a non-judgemental approach in an understanding and compassionate society, I believe that parents would be much more willing to seek help and support. Parents would receive appropriate help to resolve their own emotional and relationship issues. The vicious cycle of dysfunctional family creating dysfunctional family, generation after generation, might finally be broken.

We must place greater emphasis on improving communication. Few of us communicate with others – even our loved ones – openly and from the heart. There are very few people to whom we can truly express our feelings and vulnerability without risk of being judged. How we relate to others in our lives is well summed up by an article I read in a women's magazine years ago. A member of the social scene was asked for her definition of a boring person. She replied: 'Someone who, when you ask them how they are, they actually tell you'. How many people are there in your life with whom you feel safe enough to reveal your feelings and your vulnerability? If you have even one or two, then count your blessings.

Many people live in an emotional desert, lacking the intimacy of a loving and unconditional relationship. We need to learn how to listen to those around us, to encourage people to communicate their feelings. This came across powerfully at the end of BBC's Panorama programme on suicide in young men, *Boys Don't Cry*. Three people spoke about their deep regret that they didn't hear the pain of their loved one. A mother whose son took his own life said:

> If only I could have reached out and told him
> that he could talk and still be a man.

A second mother whose son ended his own life would have done things differently:

> I have a lot of friends who have boys the same
> age as Mark. And I have certainly spoken to
> them and said, 'Look, if things change, if the
> mood changes, listen to them, talk to them.'

A young man whose friend took his own life spoke of his own reaction:

> You know, my friend, he committed suicide a couple of years ago. I met him on the Wednesday at the post office. That Friday, I was in the studios in London and I got a phone call from me mate. He says 'How are you?' I said 'All right'. And the next thing I knew he was dead. He just threw himself off the flat later that day. And I just wish I'd asked him if *he* was all right. But we don't, do we? No one asks any more 'Are you all right? No – are you *really* all right?'

WIDER SOCIETY

Society as a whole must look at the real issues involved in 'mental illness' and suicide. For too long we have given responsibility for emotional distress, 'mental illness' and suicide to the medical profession. In doing so we have created experts who conveniently absolve society of any major role in the cause and prevention of suicide. Medical experts are spreading the message society wants to hear, a message which can be paraphrased as follows:

> Society is not in any way responsible for the suicide of our people. The cause is mental illness and society is not responsible for the creation of mental illness.

I believe that society does play a major role in causing emotional distress and suicide, and has the potential to

310

play a central part in reducing these.

In *The Interpreted World*, Ernesto Spinelli highlights society's responsibility:

> So long as a society holds on to medical models of mental illness, no examination or criticism of that society need be considered since the origins of the problem are considered to be primarily biological or genetic in nature, thereby minimising – and exculpating – any socio-environmental factors.

We must provide a comprehensive network of caring and supportive counselling services for people in emotional distress. I believe that this would provide a much more effective fire-brigade service for emotionally distressed people than that which is currently available from doctors. But providing an emergency service is not enough.

By neglecting to look at key issues around emotional distress 'mental' illness and suicide – relationships, dysfunction within families, low self-esteem, for instance – society is sweeping difficult issues under the carpet. Many people, including those who take their lives every year, are paying a high price for our failure as a society to embrace the real issues.

Millions of people lead a double life. The outward image which many young men present to the world is of hardworking, successful, important people. Happy and cheerful, they do not reveal feelings of depression, fear, or emotional vulnerability. They rarely ask for support, certainly not for emotional or psychological help. They often have a hectic social life. They seem to have it all, and are the envy of many. But the reality behind that public image may be a different story altogether. Frequently in emotional turmoil, many young men bottle it up, terrified to reveal any weaknesses which might taint their image. They fear losing the approval and acceptance of their relatives and friends. They suppress their emotions in an attempt to cope with life, which comes at them in relentless waves.

Cut off from their feelings, many young men feel cut off from people. Even in their closest relationships they may feel alone and lonely. The greater the gap – or the bigger the mask – between the public image people feel compelled to portray and the true inner world of the person, the more desperate they become. Suicide then becomes a real option which will once and for all remove them from their anguish. For years we have known that thousands of men are terrified of admitting that they have feelings – not to mention revealing them to others.

Thousands of women also live double lives; the mask they put on every day for their family, friends and others, and the person inside, often lonely, unhappy and unfulfilled. The person inside remains silent and unheard. When Jane became depressed in her late twenties, the hardest thing was the enormous isolation she experienced. There were so few people to whom she could express her real feelings. At work, and even with friends, she felt that nobody wanted to know. When people ask her how she is, she pretends. She says she is fine. She pretends most of the day. She feels so alone inside. Yet nobody at work or in her social circle knows there is anything wrong. She has learnt to become a good pretender.

Jane would love to open up about how she feels but is scared that she will be labelled a nutcase by her friends and workmates. She has good reason. She has seen how many of her friends speak about depressed people in a less than charitable fashion. Terms such as 'loony-bin' and 'nutter' are frequently exchanged at their coffee break. Jane feels so inferior, wondering if her friends would disown her if they knew how she was really feeling. She has a loving relationship with her husband, but once she leaves home to go to work, the mask goes on. She forces a smile for eight hours a day, feeling lost and alone inside.

I have noticed a trend in people's lives, particularly in women. They get married and perhaps have children. As the years go by, the needs of family and work increasingly take precedence over their own needs. They learn to stop taking care of themselves, to stop doing things for themselves. This process can occur so gradually that it goes unnoticed, like a thief in the night. Eventually the person may reach the point where there is no colour, no joy in their life and they wonder why. This insidious process can be so developed in the person's life that they need a great deal of help and encouragement to reverse it. Many times, people have said to me 'I don't know where to begin' when I am exploring with them ways of increasing the joy in their life and having their own needs met. Little wonder that many such people become depressed. They are so busy looking after other people's needs that their own needs for love, challenge, growth, fun and colour often go unmet.

Why have we created a society where people have to pretend so much? Why is helping people come to terms with emotional distress not a high priority within our society?

Why have we not created a mechanism in society to help people understand themselves better? A mechanism to help people feel safe enough to be themselves in this world?

Why have we not created a more compassionate society based on tolerance, openness and respect? A society where people can be themselves and express themselves without the ever-present fear of criticism, judgement, rejection or ridicule? Where the rights of people to hold differing views is enshrined in our society's value system? Is it really good enough that when we are greeted with 'How are you?' by people every day, we do not feel comfortable enough to tell the truth? We say 'fine', 'great', 'never better', when we really feel like screaming. The double-life dilemma rolls on.

With regard to emotional distress, 'mental illness' and suicide, we need to go back to the drawing board. We must let go of the presumed link between suicide and 'psychiatric illness'. We can create a system designed to create a deeper understanding of self-esteem, relation-ships, self-worth, understanding, emotional expression, tolerance, communication within relationships, and freedom of expression. I believe that such a network would be more acceptable and more effective than the current psychiatric service.

For years the medical profession has retained control over health policy decisions. I believe that when it comes to the issues dealt with in this book – emotional distress, 'mental illness', and suicide – the medical profession should not be given the power to veto measures simply because doctors disagree with them.

I feel that modern medicine may be too close to the

issues, too emotionally involved, to be able to stand back and take stock of itself objectively. Modern medicine's vested interest in maintaining the status quo, in ensuring that the role of 'mental illness' becomes more and more accepted by the public, may well impede the medical profession's ability to see the issues clearly and objectively.

Nor will modern medicine invite other groups – the counselling professions, for instance – to share its pedestal of expertise. Therefore, those whom the public have entrusted with the power to create change for the better – the legislators – should take whatever steps are necessary to ensure that the medical profession's monopoly of emotional pain, 'mental illness' and suicide is thoroughly and independently examined. I believe that a fundamental re-examination of emotional distress, 'mental illness' and suicide is urgently needed. In recent years we have had many investigations and tribunals into business, political and health concerns, including the Lyndsay Inquiry into the transmission of HIV through blood products. While they have cost a great deal of money, these tribunals have demonstrated that it is possible to get to the bottom of even the most intricate and complex issues. Since people's lives are more important than money, I believe that there should be a public investigation into the practice of psychiatry which should include GPs, since they deal with 90 per cent of 'psychiatric problems'. The Public Accounts Committee has done trojan work in a most cost-effective way. An independent investigation into psychiatry could be similarly set up. Given that hundreds of thousands of people use the mental health services each year, and that there is such disquiet among the public about the mental health services, such an inquiry is long overdue. Government have for decades abdicated responsibility for psychiatric research and treatment to the medical profession and the pharmaceutical industry. This abdication has allowed psychiatry to create its own brand of caring without having to account to anyone.

Intolerant attitudes are still widespread. Recently, a client of mine with depression was having coffee in a hotel lobby. At the table adjacent to hers, a group of people were discussing depression. One particularly loud man pontificated on depression to the group. According to him, depressed people are a blight on society and should be locked up. He is not alone in that view. It seems that discrimination against so-called 'mentally ill' people is common in modern Irish society.

Emotional distress is a fact of life. We cannot wish it away just because it makes us feel uncomfortable. If we are to tackle the increasing suicide rates, we must take action. The vast sums of money currently invested in psychiatry could be used to fund a caring and supportive service helping people to overcome emotional distress. Such a system must see all human beings as equal, unique and priceless. It must approach people who are emotionally distressed in a respectful way, from a viewpoint that the person's emotional distress is always understandable. Only then will we begin to provide appropriate care for emotional distress, and in doing so, reduce the suicide rate.

The stigma attached to 'mental illness' will disappear only when we realise that there is no such thing as 'mental illness', and that deep emotional distress is a natural human response to emotional pain and life-related distress. Only then will the millions of people worldwide who have been labelled 'mentally ill' have a chance of a compassionate hearing from both the general public and the caring professions. Only then will the shame and sense of inferiority these people experience so profoundly begin to disappear.

There may be a strong reaction against any such change by those with vested interests, including the medical profession. Doctors will come forward with arguments which sound logical as to why psychiatry should remain the body we must entrust with care of emotional distress. Do not be fooled. Psychiatry's track record is nothing to write home about. Psychiatry has created a niche of expertise for itself, as if possessing a special mystique, a unique wisdom and authority. This mystique limits the public's ability to examine thoroughly the true value of psychiatry's beliefs and practices. Only by demystifying psychiatry can the public identify the true value of the medical profession's approach to emotional distress, 'mental illness' and suicide. Only then can we begin to build a society and a health care system designed to meet the real needs of the people.

BIBLIOGRAPHY

American Psychiatric Association: Diagnostic and Statistical Manual of Mental Disorders, Fourth Edition, Text Revision, Washington DC: American Psychiatric Association, 2000.

Beeken, Claire, with Rosanna Greenstreet. *My Body, My Enemy.* London, Thorsons, 1997.

Breggin, Peter. *Toxic Psychiatry.* London, HarperCollins, 1993.

Breggin, Peter. *Talking Back to Prozac,* New York: St Martin's Press, 1994.

Godsen, Richard. *Punishing the Patient: How Psychiatrists Misunderstand and Mistreat Schizophrenia.* Australia, Scribe Publications, 2001.

Gould, Donald. *The Black and White Medicine Show: How Doctors Serve and Fail Their Customers.* London, Hamish Hamilton Ltd., 1985.

Humphreys, Tony. *The Power of 'Negative' Thinking.* Dublin, Gill & Macmillan, 1996.

Humphreys, Tony. *Self-esteem: The Key to Your Child's Education.* Dublin, Gill & Macmillan, 1996.

Humphreys, Tony. *The Family: Love it and Leave it.* Dublin, Gill & Macmillan, 1996.

Jamison, Kay Redfield. *An Unquiet Mind.* New York, Vintage Books, 1996.

Johnstone, Lucy. *Users and Abusers of Psychiatry*. London, Routledge, 1989.

Karon/Widener. 'The Tragedy of Schizophrenia'. *The Ethical Human Sciences and Services Journal* Vol 1 No 4: 1999. New York, Springer Publishing Company.

Laing R. D. and A. Esterson. *Sanity, Madness and the Family*. London, Pelican, 1970.

Masson, Jeffrey. *Against Therapy*. London, HarperCollins, 1997.

Medawar, Charles. *Power and Dependence*. London: Social Audit Ltd, 1992.

Medawar, Charles. The Antidepressant Web
http://www.socialaudit.org.uk.

Mendelsohn, Robert. *Confessions of a Medical Heretic*. Chicago, Contemporary Books, 1979.

Rogers, Carl. *A Way of Being*. Houghton Mifflin Company, New York, 1995. Introduction by Irvin Yalom M.D.

Rowe, Dorothy. *Depression: The Way Out of Your Prison*. London, Routledge, 1996.

Satir, Virginia. *Peoplemaking*. London, Souvenir Press, 1978.

Shaw, Fiona. *Out of Me: the Story of a Postnatal Breakdown*. London, Viking, 1997.

Shelley, Rosemary (Editor). *Anorexics on Anorexia*. London, Jessica Kingsley Publishers, 1997.

Spinelli, Ernesto. *The Interpreted World*. London, Sage Publications, 1989.

What Doctors Don't Tell You [journal], London.

INDEX